# POLITY AND PRACTICE
# IN BAPTIST CHURCHES

# BIOGRAPHY

THE author of this book is a native of Missouri. As a very young man he taught rural public schools in that State. He graduated (A..B.) at Ottawa University, Kansas, and (B. D.) at the Crozer Theological Seminary; receiving also the degree of A. M. at the University of Pennsylvania for postgraduate work. Ottawa gave him the honorary divinity doctorate in 1923. Doctor McNutt's first pastorate after leaving the theological seminary was with the Baptist church of Prospect Park, a suburb of Philadelphia. In 1916 he went to the First Baptist Church of Worcester, Massachusetts, where he remained for twelve years. His work with this large and important church was so notably successful that his theological alma mater was led to call him to its chair of Practical Theology, in 1928. He maintained this position until 1944, when he was retired by statute of age limitation. Being unwilling to withdraw from active service, Dr. McNutt accepted a call to the pastorate of the Central Baptist Church of Woodbury, New Jersey, where he remained until July 1, 1956. Thus, the present volume, in both the original and revised editions, has been written out of a rich and varied ministry. He remains "Professor Emeritus" of Crozer Seminary, and "Pastor Emeritus" of the Woodbury church.

# POLITY AND PRACTICE
# IN BAPTIST CHURCHES

*By* WILLIAM ROY McNUTT, D.D.

## FOREWORD
*By*
DOUGLAS CLYDE MACINTOSH, Ph.D., D.D., LL.D.

―――――

**THE JUDSON PRESS**

CHICAGO      PHILADELPHIA      LOS ANGELES

Gratefully dedicated

*to the*

**Prospect Hill Baptist Church**
Prospect Park, Pennsylvania

— *the*

**First Baptist Church**
Worcester, Massachusetts

*and the*

**Central Baptist Church**
Woodbury, New Jersey

three churches whose liberal attitude on matters of polity
and practice gave their minister large freedom in meeting
the needs and opportunities of this present day.

# FOREWORD

Among the many churches claiming to be Christian, where shall we find the true church of Christ, " the church of the living God "? Obviously, wherever the spirit of Christ is dominant, in whatever fellowship the will of God is being effectively done.

Whatever is right for a man to do, that presumably is God's will for his conduct. No being who willed otherwise for man could be God, and a worthy object of man's absolute worship and trust. But whatever makes most effectively for the highest ultimate well-being of mankind is what each and every human being is morally bound to find out and do. Just what this may mean in any particular situation we can progressively discover through cultivated appreciation of what is intrinsically good, better and best, and through expert knowledge of what means are most effective for realizing the best ends. The will of God for our lives is thus not to be dismissed as unknowable.

On the Christian view of God, everyone ought to be God-ruled, and not merely externally, but from within one's own will. In such obedience would be found true freedom. Religious liberty, viewed superficially and from without, may seem to be simply freedom to do as one pleases in religious matters; but, rightly understood from within, religious liberty is freely rendered obedience to the will of God. Wherever God's will is being willingly done, there is the spirit that was in Christ, and "where the Spirit of the Lord is, there is liberty." Wherever a God-ruled, individual will or church fellowship is, there the rule or kingdom of God is. Wherever Jesus went about doing good, there the kingdom of God was in the midst—for he carried it in his heart and life. The same can be said of his *true* disciples. The kingdom of God is still largely future, only because the reign of God's will in men's hearts and lives is so largely not yet a reality. "Thy kingdom come," and "Thy will be done on earth as it is in heaven," are two ways of saying the same thing.

Every individual, then, and every church ought to be a theocracy, a realm where God's will is voluntarily done. Here the sovereignty of God and the free will of man are, or would be, reconciled. [God would have all men to be saved and come to a knowledge of the truth.] He is not willing that any should perish, but that all should come to repentance. But this universal election on God's part is obviously conditional; it depends for its ratification upon man's election of God. In the spiritual realm God's sovereignty is only a glorious possibility until made actual by man's voluntary surrender to God's will and rule. Nothing can be safer, or, for the man or church that has faith in the trustworthiness of God, more logical, than such self-surrender and obedience; it is proving by works that the faith is a reality.

Wherever, as a result of whatsoever favoring influences, an individual is led to elect God as his just and gracious Sovereign, there begins a regeneration—that creation of a clean heart and that renovation of spirit of which our Bibles speak. The individual now begins to be really "competent, *under God*, in religion."

Individuals thus surrendered to the will of God and beginning to lead God-directed lives naturally gravitate into a spiritual fellowship. Discovery of the Christlike spirit of willingness to do God's will arouses a "consciousness of kind," and a church of Christ is born, a fellowship of the regenerate.

## Foreword

Our best criterion of the true church of Christ, then, must ever be its Christlike temper and its consequent effectiveness as an instrument of God's will. It will be a fellowship of the religiously competent, with every man a priest; a spiritual democracy, with every man in God a king. In other words, the church will have a right to be a democracy only because and only in so far as it is at the same time a theocracy, a realm where God's will is recognized and done.

From this it will be seen to be imperative that the local Christian fellowship, like the individual Christian man, be left independent enough of ecclesiastical and political authority to be free to find out and follow the will of God as the only absolute and all-sufficient law. Opinions of other Christian individuals and decisions of other ecclesiastical bodies should be treated with consideration and respect; however, no such expression of judgment or will can be consistently accepted as final and authoritative legislation, but only as friendly advice. Freedom to organize for effective Christian service must be conceded, but in all this the right of the individual and the local fellowship independently to seek to discover and do the will of God must also be allowed. Similarly, governmental laws and regulations can be acquiesced in by the consistently Christian individual or church only in so far as they do not prescribe conduct that conflicts with the manifest will of God, defined in terms of moral duty and the highest well-being of mankind.

From this spiritually free and Christian point of view the Scriptures of our faith may be read, not only as record and product of great historic religious experiences, but also as record and product of great revelations of the spirit, will and power of God, operating in those experiences of individuals and of the primitive church. And just because the Scriptures are the record and product of revelation, they bring to us the permanent possibility of a similar revelation of God in our own religious experience today.

Ritual acts practised by the primitive churches, such as baptism—symbolizing the beginning of a new life in conscious fellowship with Christ—and the Lord's Supper—symbolizing communion with God and with fellow Christians through Christ—may well be retained; but they must not be allowed to degenerate into something irrational, unspiritual, or sub-Christian. Not only must they not be made into semimagical substitutes for the actual experience of the grace of God which comes through self-surrender and faith; they must not even be taken as legalistic requirements, punctilious observance of which can in and of itself amount to meritorious obedience. Baptism and the ritual of communion are of the nature of dramatic profession of faith and promise of obedience. As actions they sometimes speak louder than words, but what they say is pledge rather than performance. Consequently, the observance of these ancient Christian rites —psychologically valuable for Christian experience, as they should be, and often are—ought never to be put on the same level with Christian experience, Christian faith and Christian purpose, as *indispensable* preconditions of fellowship in the Christian church.

Because I believe the author of this book on Baptist polity and practice to be in essential accord with the convictions which I, as a Baptist, have here expressed, I am happy and consider myself honored in the privilege of writing this introductory foreword.

THE DIVINITY SCHOOL OF
YALE UNIVERSITY.

DOUGLAS C. MACINTOSH.

# CONTENTS

# INTRODUCTION

FOR FIRST AND SECOND PRINTINGS.

Since the polity of Baptist churches, like a living organism, is constantly in process of changing and developing, each decade requires a fresh study thereof. Notably is review essential to the membership of the churches lest the people find themselves out of step with denominational growth. This volume claims to be such a survey, and moreover is written with a view to meeting the need of study and discussion groups within the local church, community schools of religion, summer conferences, and the like.

The author has studiously avoided making *ex cathedra* pronouncements concerning fixity of polity, for the simple reason that these are inappropriate in the description of that which lives and hence is characterized by fluidity and motion. Moreover, there has been avoidance of unfounded generalizations as to this or that item of polity. Many practices are sectional, yet are distinctly Baptist; for example, close communion, a practice of most Southern Baptists, and mixed membership, rather widespread among English Baptists.

Grateful acknowledgment is made for constructive criticisms and valuable suggestion on the part of Milton G. Evans, D. D., LL. D., president emeritus of Crozer Theological Seminary; Rev. Rittenhouse Neisser, director of the Crozer Extension Course in the same institution, and Rev. Howard Wayne Smith, D. D., all of whom read the manuscript. Thanks are offered likewise to many friends who freely answered inquiries regarding certain matters of polity; and to publishers who have granted the privilege of reference or quotation.

## The Point of View

Polity has been defined as "that general or fundamental system or organization of an institution, as determined by the basic theory on which it is built." The careful student of the polities of the several branches of the Christian church cannot accept wholly that definition. Its implications are those of the skeleton rather than of the organism, the structural rather than the living and growing. A given polity is a living thing, animating the structural—unless, indeed, life has departed, leaving a corpse; and even so what remains is the product of life processes. Polity may be defined more aptly as the habitual, the approved and somewhat fixed ways of acting. For instance, Presbyterian polity is constituted of those habitual modes of action, those habitual methods and procedures, according to which the living church expresses its life.

However, one phase of that definition quoted above is acceptable, namely, the "basic theory on which it is built." For each polity holds within itself a creative principle by virtue of which it grows its own peculiar characteristics. A certain creative principle predetermines one organism to become a horse, while another creative principle comes to animate existence in an elephant. Just so, the monarchial principle begets a monarchial polity and the democratic principle a congregational polity. We define polity, therefore, as that body of the more basic, habitual ways and procedures—all of which are under the guidance of a given creative principle—by means of and in accordance with which a living church manifests its life and projects its ministry.

# Introduction

These ways and procedures are evolved by the biological processes of trial and error, or experimentation. Many ways are tried out, some of which are rejected as unprofitable while others are finally raised to a place of more or less permanence. Let an illustration serve us. Into a test-tube an experimenter drops a number of ingredients and then watches carefully the chemical action that follows. When action is complete he observes a precipitate, the result of his experiment. Polity, so to speak, is a precipitate; it is that which remains after experimentation with many plans and programs, methods and procedures designed to guide group action.

By this route history delivers to us a number of polities: Monarchial, Aristocratic, Episcopal, Consistorial, Presbyterial, Congregational, and what we may designate the Eclectic. These are illustrated respectively by the Western Church, the Eastern Church, the Church of England, the Lutheran Church (on the Continent, particularly), the Presbyterian Church, the Baptist churches, and the Methodist Church. Of course, these polities are widely variant, evolved, as they have been, under control of their respective creative principles. Some are old, others young; and in turn they bear the marks of age, maturity, and youth.

It is pertinent to make note of the fact that the student of these polities finds each to have served well its constituency as an adequate means of expressing the life of the living church. Each bears the distinctive marks of the age in which it was born, together with the marks of the century to which it has ministered. For instance, the curtain had scarcely dropped on the apostolic age when the stage was set to reveal a developing monarchial polity. How could it have been otherwise, since the youthful church was moving into that monarchial political order, dominated by the Roman Empire? Perhaps a church that was to minister to a society of monarchial type would show wisdom in growing a monarchial polity. At any rate that is what came to pass. And who would hazard the opinion that some other type of polity, say the congregational, would have served better the needs of the age? Whatever be one's answer to these questions, the fact remains that each type continues to serve well large groups of Christians in their organizational life.

The relation of a developing polity to the general historical movement of a given era is finely illustrated by the Presbyterian type, whose distinctive characteristic is that of representative government and control. Its development began with the European Reformation, which, as is common knowledge, was merely one phase of the Renaissance which was to strangely modify the entire social structure of Europe. It marked the beginning of the march away from monarchy and toward democracy; Presbyterianism arose, expressing in church life a happy mean between these two extremes. It is a polity distinctively the child of its age. In America the Presbyterian polity is almost exactly the religious counterpart of the federal government of the United States. It is republicanism, rather than democracy, in church life. It seems clear that the major influence in the birth and growth of each of the historic polities lies in the predominant social organization, or movement, of its particular age. Vindication for each type, as an afterthought, has been found in the New Testament. (A matter discussed in Chapter I.)

If the foregoing statement needs modification in any respect it is in regard to congregational polity. Like others its germ seed sprang into life among the young churches of the New Testament period. But the climate of that ancient world was inhospitable to the tender plant of democracy wherever it lifted itself. Nevertheless, it found those who loved its promise of freedom and who consequently hid it and kept it alive. For fifteen centuries it was a submerged and outlawed growth, the particular care and hope of small, heretical sects and nonconformist groups. In the fulness of time, however, the zephyrs of democracy began to blow across the face of the Western world gradually tempering its climate toward springtime. Cautiously the plant of democracy—congregationalism in the church—was set out into the warming sun. It took deeper root and began with some boldness to show itself. The story of its growth is romantic, and known to all. However, we cannot escape the fact that a democratic polity of church came along with the age of democracy. Like all other polities, its development has been indigenous to a particular period of history, and it is but one flower in the garden of that age.

A world-figure among English statesmen cheered millions of Baptists when he declared, " This is Baptist day." His meaning is clear; he was saying that we have swung definitely into a democratic age, and in such those churches which have a genius for democracy ought to make a great contribution. The Baptist churches constitute not only the largest manifestation of congregationalism in the history of Christianity, but at the same time the most extensive experiment in pure democracy in all history. These facts are sufficient to focus attention upon the polity of these thousands of free and independent churches as they work out their procedures and perform their ministry. Therefore this volume constitutes a study of the rise and development of Baptist polity; notably that of the churches of this name in the United States.

### Topics for Group Discussion

1. Arrive at a clear idea, by group thinking, of what is meant by church polity. Formulate a definition of polity.

2. Name the various types of polity, discussing the meaning of the " creative principle " in each, and showing specific phases wherein this formative principle has done its work.

3. Should a polity be thought of in terms of an organization—or of an organism? Why so?

4. Discuss how a certain type of polity, for instance that of the Baptist churches, has come to be what it is today. Is it a fossilized structure, or is it fluid and changing? Give illustrations of fossilization, or fluidity, as the case may be.

5. Take up one of the historic polities and discover its relation to history and to Scripture. Which is the more influential and formative?

6. What is the Christian attitude for a group to take toward polities, other than that of the church to which its members belong? Why such an attitude?

### Books Worth Consulting

Encyclopedia Britannica, Articles on " Baptists," " Presbyterians," etc.

Newbigin, Leslie, *The Household of God: Lectures on the Nature of the Church.* The Friendship Press, New York, 1954.

# Introduction

Newman, Albert H., *A History of the Baptist Churches in the United States.* The American Baptist Publication Society, Philadelphia, 1898.

New Testament.

Vedder, Henry C., *A Short History of the Baptists.* The American Baptist Publication Society, Philadelphia, 1907.

Webster's Dictionary.

Writings of early influential Baptists, such as Andrew Fuller, and old minutes of associations.

## PRACTICAL SUGGESTIONS

1. The discussion method of teaching comes into increasing favor. The church school teacher, or minister, who can use the method wisely has found the way to creative teaching. Results of discussion are more than the sum total of the thought of all the individuals; it is that plus something, and it is the " plus " which makes real discussion significant. Often a dull pupil will snap into mental alertness in the give-and-take of discussion. Try it, persistently! The " Topics for Discussion " are framed to provoke such mental invigoration.

2. Every Baptist should aim to be genuinely intelligent about the polity of the Baptist churches. Every wide-awake minister knows the danger that lurks in the uninformed church-member; he is so apt in acting from prejudice rather than from actual knowledge.

This volume is designed to be used by groups willing to pay the price of coming to know the structural life of the Baptist churches.

3. One instance will suffice to indicate the significance of polity: the type of the program of the Stockholm Conference in the year 1925. It was a program dealing

with "Life and Works"; it dared not touch polity at any point. Polity could not be mentioned when all Christendom met in conference! Fortunately, real matters could be discussed: the quality of life demanded of the Christian, and the kind of ministry to the world which must challenge him. Though all present-day polities have been created out of group experiences, these have come to be thought of as sacred, and more important than life and ministry!

4. It would be most wholesome should this study inspire the group to go on to make at least a casual study of the polities of other bodies of Christians, with a view to appreciation and evaluation of their virtues.

## INTRODUCTION

### FOR REVISED EDITION

A main thesis of this book is that the polity of our Baptist churches is continually changing. Because this polity of change has wrought much since 1935, there is need of considerable revision. This has been undertaken in order to place in the hands of the reader or the student a volume which is up to date and authoritative.

Many newer books have been added to chapter lists as well as to the comprehensive bibliography at the end of the volume. The index has been greatly enlarged by adding new subjects and cross references that make the total contents more readily available. The philosophy of "Polity and Practice" remains unchanged, but there are emendations that will make it more serviceable.

In these revisions the author has been assisted greatly by the knowledge and counsel of the Rev. W. Clinton Powers, of Denison University.

# I

## NEW TESTAMENT POLITY

Baptists have frequently characterized themselves as " Bible Christians." It is fair to say that they have uniformly desired to be such, and that the characterization approximates accuracy. The difficulty is to determine the precise photograph of the New Testament Christian, and then to find convincing evidence that all Baptists resemble such a composite photograph. However, this people have diligently searched the Scriptures that they might find direction for both individual conduct and group action; and having found it—as they thought—their course was henceforth determined. Though they may have hoped for a guidance at once positive and unabridged, they have seldom been able to discover more than " a *sufficient* guide to faith and practice."

Among other objects of their quest was to find the New Testament church, and apprehend its life and polity. They doubtless hoped to come upon an actual, true picture of this church. That such existed was never questioned in the earlier days and rarely is at present. Even so, there is no evidence that they ever announced to the world a discovery beyond " a sufficient guide " in matters of church and polity. Though they sought a blue-print, they found only a sketchy outline. Instead of a detailed drawing of foundations and superstructure by the Master's own hand, they have witnessed bands of disciples conscientiously attempting to actualize in an institution his dream of a church. They have found them here and there organizing themselves freely after the dictates of safety, mutual aid and edification, the wise administration of charity, the more certain holding of their inheritance in Christ, the more effective spread of his blessed gospel of life, and the furtherance of the Kingdom which he would establish.

These infant churches were democratically organized and administered. Their incipient polity seemed uniform and unvarying, simple in outline, yet adequate to the needs at hand. Each was a unit in itself and as such was independent of any or all others. Each chose from its own number such leaders, or set apart for special ministry such workers, as its situation and local needs demanded. These were variously designated as deacons, elders, pastors, teachers, evangelists, and prophets; but they maintained a common status, namely, that of members of the local church. In other words, there was no official elevation. In addition to these chosen leaders the churches gladly received and heard other brethren, honored of all, who circulated among the scattered churches as friends and counselors, but neither claiming nor exercising authority. Thus have Baptists read this divine charter of their churches, a charter written to define a polity of democracy and independency, of freedom in and loyalty to Jesus Christ as the one and only Head of the church.

Arresting, however, is the fact that every other denomination of Christian people has likewise found the roots of its polity in this same New Testament. How is this historic fact to be accounted for? Each denomination has produced men of profound scholarship who have, in all honesty, vindicated their particular thesis to the entire satisfaction of their respective group. But there remains the significant consideration, as Canon Streeter [1] points out, that no one of these has ever been able at the same time both to vindicate his own position and destroy the claim of others to Scriptural polity. Each church has seemed to say, " We are right regardless of the claims of others," and has then gone on its way with such charity toward others as it were possible to muster.

Manifestly all cannot be wholly correct in their respective positions. It may be granted that it is within the range of the possible that some one of the denominations has all the truth regarding New Testament polity on its side, and that all others are in error; possible, but hardly probable. It may be that each is partly right and partly wrong in its position, that each holds error mixed with its truth; at least the error of assuming that those who differ are perverse in their particular error. May it not be that the assumption of a single revealed type of polity in the New Testament cannot be maintained? Can it be that these scriptural records actually bear testimony to a variance in polity from place to place, and as the years passed? Such questions press for answer, making necessary a restudy of the documents in order to determine, if possible, the validity of the position of Baptists (and others) relative to the New Testament church and their strict adherence to that revealed type of polity.

It has been pointed out many times that the world into which Christianity was born and in which its churches were being established was a world prolific of associations, societies, clubs, guilds, and all the rest. In addition, there was the synagogue, familiar to every Jewish convert and known to every Gentile disciple. It is inconceivable that these environing organizations should not have affected

[1] *The Primitive Churches,* by B. H. Streeter.   Scribner's.

the polity of the new churches. As a matter of fact, they practically determined it. The synagogue with its democratic organization profoundly influenced both their form and spirit. It is almost unknown in the history of social institutions that men create their constitutions *de novo*. These churches are no exception in this regard. They did organize " charity," or philanthropy, on a new scale and scope; yet even here they found existing fertilizing suggestions. In other words, the polity of the New Testament churches is eclectic on the structural side. The significant matter is that into borrowed framework there was breathed the soul of a new and marvelously radiant life.

Let us turn to the documents, to the New Testament itself, for the light they may give as we seek answer to our queries. Coming to a study of the church founded in Jerusalem, one immediately discovers that the item of charity is to the fore, and that almoners of funds were chosen to make distribution. These almoners are called deacons, or servers. Two considerations are to be noted, first, that current associations also had groups of those who served; and second, that these deacons were chosen when the need arose and to meet that particular need. The need antedated and produced the " server."

To the outsider, this church was just another religious association. Like the others it was working out its way of doing things, its polity. There is no doubt that its guiding spirit was at the outset democratic. The Seven were chosen, or elected, by the Christian community. The procedure was, in this case, thoroughly congregational. The duties of these men were at first very simple and concrete. But we need not suppose that serving tables and giving out charity remained their only ministry. New needs created new opportunities to serve, and evoked new methods. Thus in time grew a considerable body of proper ways for doing things, i. e., a polity for the board of deacons.

But this church was active beyond the work of the Seven. The Twelve were teaching and preaching. Among those who wrought here, however, we catch a photograph of a man, than whom for our purpose the sacred writings yield none more revealing, James the brother of our Lord. Though once skeptical of Jesus' claims, he later became an ardent disciple. Since he was by relationship able to continue the Davidic line, the situation was strikingly set for his advance. And James was not a man to scorn such an opportunity. He added to this inherent prestige accorded by the Christian community a conciliatory attitude toward the old religion, its temple, and its legalistic demands. In every sense he proved himself a practical ecclesiastic, wise almost to the point of craftiness. There are certain convincing indications that there developed early no inconsiderable rivalry between James and Peter for the place of leadership. Had not the church at Jerusalem perished with the destruction of that city, the whole Christian movement might well have come to center about James and his Messianic line, rather than Peter and his successors at Rome. In other words, the New Testament gives a clear and definite silhouette of James exercising the authority of a bishop of the monepiscopal type; a type which by the turn into the second century was not uncommon.

Very different was the case with Paul and the churches established by him and his helpers. Over these he continued to exercise a close watch-care. By visitations, messengers, and epistles he never suffered a break of pastoral relationship between himself and these infant churches, his spiritual offspring. He was to each like a father whose love remains as untarnished gold. Never once did he assume to exercise official authority of any sort over them. Doubtless to do so was not without the range of temptation for him. The churches were composed of " babes," untutored in the things of Christ, and too often unweaned from the sins of contemporaneous life. They were unable to digest the strong meat of the gospel's demands, and had to be fed on " milk." That Paul, vexed by the inconsistent living of many in his churches, sometimes wished for a brief day of authority, is easily imagined. But this he could not seize and employ. He had burned all bridges behind when he turned his face away from the law and set out toward spiritual freedom. In all parts he had been a preacher of liberty in Christ. In such liberty he had laid the foundations of his churches. By the lyre of liberty he had charmed and won most of his converts. And now, whatever the provocation, he would not and could not assume the authority which would negate the even tenor of all his teaching.

In this dilemma, the ideal of liberty being its one horn and the practical necessity for a strong, guiding hand being the other, Paul took a middle position. In all the churches he appointed elders. Just who these men were, how they were chosen, and what authority, if any, they were to exercise, is not clear. One may conjecture, since they arose to meet the pressing need for closer organization and more definite guidance, that they were given at least a fixed, official status. To note that fact, together with the express statement that " they appointed them elders in all the churches," is to take cognizance of an important step in the development of the advancing polity of the Pauline churches. This is doubly significant if *he appointed* these elders. In such case the great apostle by so much is observed receding from the position of absolute local autonomy.

But there were churches in Asia founded by other hands. What can be learned about their polity from Scripture? We may look in upon their workings through a rather clear window, namely the Johannine epistles. The author, who signs himself " the Elder," wrote in the neighborhood of the year A. D. 100; probably a little before. The first letter is general and was written with the evident intent of being circulated among a group of churches; churches over which the Elder had superintendence of some sort. Of just what sort is clearly reflected in the third, the shortest and most direct of these writings. It is written to one Gaius, a prominent member of some one of the churches, now presided over by Diotrephes. The point of the letter is an attack upon this local pastor " who loveth to have preeminence."

Let us scrutinize this quarrel. The Elder was evidently dispatching among the churches under his care certain brethren, teachers or evangelists. He had written in advance letters of commendation. Diotrephes had replied, refusing to permit these men to come before his people. This act had divided his church, some clinging to him while others took sides with the Elder. So violent had this storm become that some of the latter had been put out of the church. The Elder was led openly to join with the minority group in opposing their minister. The epistle is addressed to this minority, of which Gaius was doubtless the leader.

The foregoing sets forth the facts in the case as revealed by the letter itself. These facts are explained only when we know the Elder—surely John the Elder—to be a man in authority over a group of churches. Diotrephes had the temerity to call in question that authority with the result that the bishop was greatly nettled. The point of his authority was his crazy-bone—and it had been struck. Third John was written in heat and irritation. The writer was in all probability the Bishop of Ephesus, and by virtue of his position in the large city had extended his sway over surrounding churches in smaller towns. He was a man of authority. And Diotrephes, to whom we have referred as local minister, really exercised more authority than is becoming a mere pastor of a congregation; he not only "loveth to have the preeminence" (like the Elder himself) but "neither doth he himself receive the brethren, and forbiddeth them that would, and casteth them out of the church." This looks like the picture of a man of authority, for does he not exercise the power of excommunication? And let us remember that all this happened at the end of the first Christian century.

It remains to call attention to one more item of polity among the New Testament churches. We refer to the committee, or governing board, of *presbuteroi;* literally a group of the older men; though, as Harnack indicates, they were not always necessarily old men, the term being a title of honor bestowed upon officials. Such a committee, or board, was in general operation in the churches. It constituted a quite universal element of their polity. The work of such a board was that of general guidance of affairs within a given church, without authority in the strict sense. It is interesting that the singular number is not used of such an official; the presbyter remained a member of a group. Not so with the elder and the bishop, both of whom rose to individuality as officials in or among the churches.

Our purpose would not be advanced by a further study of the polity of the churches which have their beginning in the New Testament period. The foregoing pages serve to make certain facts stand out with undeniable clarity:

1. Polity, in the New Testament, is a living thing. It is an organism growing in accordance with emerging needs. It makes free adaptation to the particular environment.

2. The men who live in these documents as founders and leaders of churches are not conscious of any revealed pattern for their guidance. They are workmen who freely pioneer in matters of constitutions, administration, procedure, and method. They are builders of a new institution, builders inspired by the Master's dream of a glorious church; men who are under bond to create a temple becoming the life and spirit of the Lord Jesus Christ.

3. As a natural result, uniformity is absent. As between the Jerusalem church and the churches born of Paul's labors, polity is widely divergent. What a gulf we find between those Syrian churches—offspring of Antioch—with their apostles, prophets and teachers, and those presided over by the Elder, Bishop of Ephesus! Here are both the freedom of democracy and the control of the monarchial bishopric—at least the attempted control.

4. Different tendencies are apparent, tendencies which during the next century, the second, make all but uniform stride toward some sort of episcopacy.

5. The conflict between what we may call spiritual guidance, as over against official control, is already in bold

relief. And so certain is the drift from the former toward the later that even the casual student may discern the movement.

6. Polity almost exclusively retains its fluid state; the process of freezing into fixity is discernible in very few instances.

In these conclusions reside sufficient grounds for the claim of many bodies of Christians that they find their polity in the New Testament. *Varying* polities *are* there, in embryo. The roots of the Congregational, the Presbyterian, and the Episcopal lie exposed; others may be, and have been found by a bit of digging!

Finally let it be observed, in confirmation of Baptist polity, that there was in the New Testament period a very wide exercise of direction and control by the Christian community itself. This was achieved through the group meeting and by committees or boards of presbyters. Moreover, it is certain that there was a very large degree of independence among the widely scattered churches. It should again be noted that the polity of these churches was wholly liquid, and was being freely fashioned as the years went on. This, in fact, is the one and only constant we can discover, aside from a warm concern for Christ and his cause, by a study of the documents that hold the secrets of the Christian churches' germinal polities.

## Topics for Group Discussion

1. Whether or not Baptist churches are " New Testament churches." If they are, are some other churches also " New Testament churches "?
2. See what can be found in the New Testament and elsewhere about the sources of the growing churches' polities; are they wholly original?

3. Make a list of all the types of ministry—prophets, elders, deacons, etc.—mentioned in the New Testament, determining their respective functions and relationships.
4. From a study of the New Testament try to form a composite picture of each—James, Peter, and Paul. Bring out similarities and contrasts.
5. Is there a uniform, revealed type of polity in the New Testament?

### BOOKS WORTH CONSULTING

Champion, L. G., *The Church of the New Testament*. The Kingsgate Press, London, 1951.

Latourette, Kenneth Scott, *A History of Christianity*. Harper and Brothers, New York, 1953.

Newman, Albert H., *A Manual of Church History*. The Judson Press, Philadelphia, 1903.

New Testament.

### PRACTICAL SUGGESTIONS

1. Make much of the Board of Deacons. Enlarge its ministry as opportunity comes, working out a schedule of service that will challenge the best that is in the finest men in the church. On the other hand, avoid a program of regular and fixed small matters, such as pall on real men.

2. In like manner let the *presbuteroi,* whom we may call the church trustees, be held in honor and given large responsibility. It is their task to lead the whole people in generously financing the church and all its work.

3. Educate the church-membership to believe in and exercise its liberty to work out its own polity as new situa-

tions arise. This will keep the people alert and pioneering, and save them from that type of fixity that hampers action in the face of need, and thereby invites palsy and death.

4. The wise minister will avoid any show of authority among his people; neither will he calmly tolerate it in others. A Baptist church is conceived in democracy, and the genius thereof must be maintained. Strangely, there are ministers and laymen who are strong for Baptist democracy—providing they can boss it. From the time of " the Elder " down to the present, the untoward show of authority has bred trouble. Let One only be in authority among us, even Christ.

5. Encourage first-hand study of Scripture on the part of the people. Some specific subject like, " Polity of the New Testament Churches," will give purpose and direction to such study. Individual findings, carefully checked by group findings, and by competent biblical scholars, will go far to establish the church-membership in a sound appreciation of Scripture and at the same time make them immune to strange and specious interpretations.

## II

## THE BAPTIST DOCTRINE OF CHURCH

The polity of Baptist churches, like that emergent in the New Testament, is alive. It is not unlike an organism: it is born in simplicity, develops toward complexity, and thus describes a life history. The likeness may be carried farther. A given organism passes through the various phases of its life in accordance with some inner principle or law. This hidden dynamic, unseen by the observer, predetermines the life history. When it is unfolded it will accord with this compelling, inescapable urge. It is precisely thus with a church polity that is permitted to grow up. In contradistinction to manufactured polity—the " handed-down " variety—the polity of the Baptist churches has known the pangs of birth, the vicissitudes of growing up, the strength of maturity and the rheumatic inflexibility that comes with the multiplying years.

The womb which gives birth to Baptist polity and at the same time endows it with its directive life principle is doctrinal. It is the offspring of a tenet which in small compass constitutes the major contribution of Baptist thought to the Christian world. We refer to the creative idea that the individual is competent in all matters of religion; has within himself by divine gift and right those capacities that make him competent to meet all the demands with which genuine religion confronts him. In these affairs he has no need for priest to intercede on his behalf; he is able to make his own approach to God. He has no inescapable need of church to bring him salvation or mediate to him divine grace; he possesses capacity to attain these directly through Jesus Christ, who is the one and only High Priest, the one and only mediator of salvation. Each and every man, says the Baptist, is sufficiently competent in all this realm, for the simple reason that the God with whom he has to do thus created him.

It is the doctrine of soul competency that produced the Baptist doctrine of church. Assuming the validity of the former, there is bound to follow a doctrine of church which will nurture, grow, and edify the competent soul. Moreover, as the idea of soul competency necessarily gives rise to a compatible doctrine of church, so also does the latter immediately give birth to an infant polity after its own kind. Let us turn at once, therefore, to an examination of the doctrine of soul competency, mother of the churches and their polity.

In the first instance, this doctrine greatly exalts man— even the humble, average man. However lowly he may be rated by his fellows, he carries in himself the high potential of competency. He may be regarded by those who know him as an outcast, but his Father has not cast him out; he has made his child competent in the realm of highest possible human attainment, the realm of religion. He may be numbered among the poor, but God has endowed him with surpassing riches of being. Neighbors may have little confidence in him, but He who made him believes in him and places high hope in him. Verily, no other doctrine held in favor among men so greatly puts resiliency and adventure into the hearts of men.

By virtue of a divinely bestowed competency it follows that men are free. They claim liberty as an inalienable right. God in his benign wisdom has bestowed such, and none dare take it away. The soul that is competent is likewise free. As corollary follows proposition in geometry, so freedom of soul follows competency. They cannot be separated in thought, and must not be divorced in organized religion. To do so is to strangle man and fly into the face of God. Any individual or group, any institution, though it appropriate the robes of sanctity, that sets itself to abridge or deny the exercise of soul liberty is anathema in the eyes of the understanding mind. Thus the doctrine of competency nurtures and safeguards the freedom of men in the sphere of religion.

Voluntariness, a term much heard in the councils of Baptists, comes to be claimed with insistence. Those who are by divine endowment competent in matters of religion, may or may not exercise their capacities. They may do wholly as they choose. Such may even deny or curse God and remain entirely within the realm of inalienable right. No compulsion may be exercised by any one. Show of authority—with drive in it—is an unwarranted assumption of power. Competent souls will have none of it. The will of man represents a holy of holies which even God respects, and so men and the institutions of men *must* respect it. Freedom of conscience in the exercise of will transcends all human arrangements. Conduct within the realm of religion must bear the stamp of voluntariness, else it is " bastard and not a son." The story of Baptists in their demand for a recognition of this principle makes one of the most interesting chapters in all the history of religion. A story not ours here to record, however.

The doctrine of competency reaches into the life of the individual with significant results. Among these is a personal responsibility of peculiar weight. To multitudes it is a frightful responsibility, to escape which they seek a refuge of safety and release. Men, by the logic of this doctrine they espouse, hold in their own hands the destiny of their immortal souls. The love of God has provided "salvation in his Son," but men may reject the proffer. That is to say, the God who has created man competent respects that competency to the last degree. He may choose to exercise suasion, but coercion he will never employ. The responsibility is man's to choose, "with all to gain—or all to lose."

We cannot refrain from the observation that the fruit which hangs on the extreme branches men often elect to pass by. The trunk doctrine of competency, which exalts and sets free, multitudes embrace, but the fruit of responsibility is a bitter apple which they cast aside. To change the figure, as men fleeing from the raging wind take refuge in a cave, so to escape the logical implicates of competency many seek shelter in some theory or doctrine or institution which will assume or bear their responsibility for them. But God, we may rest assured, recognizes no such comfortable subterfuge. By the way of competency he would grow sons and daughters, and in that way his holy feet are set to the end of the ages.

Competency reposes authority in religion within the individual. It sets each man on a throne which holds absolute sway over his own realm. And he may not, for any reason, abdicate; he rules by divine right and appointment. God will not release him from his sacred charge. This may seem a hard doctrine and one difficult to receive, but the Baptist position does not blink it. Men must heed the injunction, "Work out your own salvation with fear and trembling"; a ringing challenge of the great apostle of that freedom which competency breeds.

## The Baptist Doctrine of Church

Let it be added that while one may not abdicate his throne, he may call to his side those who have counsel to give. Such he may hear, and from them take little or much, as seems good in his sight. If wise, he will wish to hear the wisdom of others. He will consult the experience of those who appear to rule well their own estates; he will ask history, science, art and other fields of human knowledge for their word to him; he will sit at the feet of many who claim to know God and his ways; he will read books and the Book for the light they bring, illumining his own heart and mind; he will walk with Jesus, prophet and Light of the World; and he will listen with a deep yearning for the still small voice of Him who has made man competent to hear divine messages. He will seek and hear many counselors, but in favor of no one of these may he abdicate. He may accept the will of God—so far as it is in his power to ascertain it—and in fact is morally blameworthy if he refuses to accept it and act upon it.

Competency has been and continues to be a living force in the hands of Baptists. It consistently throws the whole weight of a creative idea against every form of legalism in religion, it will have no intercourse with sacramentalism of any sort, it eschews creedalism in every form, and lifts a hue and cry at every indication that civil government intends to make inroads into religious territory. It confronts all these and all such with resistance because they are each some form of, or threat of, authority from without looking toward the limiting of the free exercise of competency. The now famous Douglas C. Macintosh affair is a case in point in recent days. The government may not preempt a man's conscience in advance. One may not abdicate, though his government demand it. So says the doctrine of competency—and so says a weighty minority of the Supreme Court of the United States!

In the foregoing pages we have hastily traced out that lower stratum of Baptist doctrine (not implying that competency is today held exclusively by Baptists—we rejoice that it is otherwise—though historically it is a Baptist contribution) which gives rootage and upward thrust to the polity of the Baptist churches.  Superimposed on that stratum is the doctrine of the church held by this people.

Though one did not have three centuries of history as authority and guide, one could predict that when a Baptist church did come into being it would be, in some vital sense, a "competent" church.  And so it is.  Every local church is held to be competent in and of itself, to bear the whole witness of Christ to the whole world.  It has no need of commission or authority save that received from Him who dwells in the church and is its only Head and Lord.  The church so conceived is an organized band of disciples of Christ.  In the exercise of divinely inbred competency each individual has *chosen* Christ as Lord, with the consequent regeneration of his own life. Competency is thereby given new insight and inspiration.  Under Christ each becomes his own priest in his own right; hence the tenet, "the priesthood of all believers."  In witness of regeneration and faith in all its meanings for the Christian life, each has been baptized in water.  Hence Baptists define a church as follows:

*A church is an organized group of the baptized disciples of Christ, regenerate by and through him, made priests unto God by his appointment, recognizing him alone as Head, and purposing to keep their hearts warm in allegiance to him, their Lord, to culture their souls in his graces, and to spread the good news about him through all the earth.*

Such a church is an independent unit democratically functioning in cooperation with other groups of disciples to enlarge the reign of God in the hearts of men everywhere; cooperating, in other words, for the extension of the kingdom of heaven on earth. Hence the church and the Kingdom are not synonymous. A church is an *agent* of that Kingdom, which is as wide as the reign of Christ in the hearts and affairs of men. The church exists therefore, not for itself, but as a means committed to God for the furtherance of his purposes on earth. In proportion as it yields itself a loyal and effective instrument in his hand, is it a true church. To be thus effective it must make itself rich in its own inner life of faith; hence the local program for the culture of the membership in all that pertains to godliness.

Now out of these two doctrinal strata, that of soul competency and that of the free association of believers as a church, springs polity. As soon as a church is born it begins to act, to manifest life. Like any organism it begins to " behave "; and it does so in accordance with its own guiding principle. Hence a Baptist church will act like a Baptist church. It will behave in a way to safeguard the competency of its members and nurture their souls, that they may actualize in life the potencies that are within them. That behavior in all its varied forms and manifestations constitutes the polity of that church. As churches multiply, and ways of acting become more or less uniform and more or less established, there results a body of polity. This is made up of practices and ways of doing things which the churches have found to be good for their guidance and the furtherance of their work.

## Polity and Practice in Baptist Churches

A church constituted by individuals who believe themselves endowed with competency in religion, and brought into being for the furtherance of their purposes—as in Christ they conceive them—such a church, by the very logic of its nature, must behave democratically. Any other type of organization than the congregational, democratic, would be inimical to its health. It would violate the inherent constitution conceived to be fundamental in each of its members. If the individual member is to grow, he must have large scope in which to exercise his soul competency. Young eagles cannot learn to fly when confined in a cage, nor young deer to leap when restrained by the high walls of the zoological garden. No more can the young Christian be expected to grow when the wings of his free soul are hurt by the scissors born of laws and the inhibitions begotten of fears. No authority, therefore, which may be conceived to interfere with health-begetting freedom can be at all permitted. Such organization or polity as does come into being by sheer necessity of group purpose must rest lightly as the dawn upon the vibrant, naked soul of the individual. He is master of all polity and must never be mastered by it. Polity is made for man and not man for polity. He that was created in the image of God must not be bound by the cords of organization. Hence the ideal of each Baptist church is the attainment of a pure democracy in all its ways. And such a democracy has been and is the first strong plank in the platform of the churches that bear this honored name.

The jealousy with which Baptists from the beginning have guarded their freedom of soul is indicated by the fact that they bind themselves together by a voluntary Covenant, one given by each to the other members of the church. For the same reasons that the Mayflower Compact was drawn on board that historic vessel, has every group of Baptists covenanted to walk together in the life and ministry of godliness, as exemplified in Christ their Lord. Thus they contract to be bound by enriching and ennobling loyalties to Christ and to each other. From such a covenant relation one may withdraw whenever he chooses; and should a member break faith by unrighteous conduct, the manner of expulsion takes the form of " withdrawal of the hand of Christian fellowship." This action on the part of the church recognizes the offender's liberty to act unrighteously if he so chooses; hence it follows him no farther than the threshold over which he has passed in disfellowship. His absolute freedom of action, limited only by his voluntary entrance into covenant, is now restored by his own acts of disavowal. So that in reality the man who thus breaks faith puts himself out of the church. Hence is vindicated the high principle that a church which cherishes liberty for itself may not act to restrain another, even though he once was fellowshiped by it.

Democratic behavior, whether in individual or group, carries in its bosom the seed of independency. Democracy bears its fruitage in this instance in independency of action on the part of a church. Each is regarded a law unto itself. The " independency of the local church " is a cardinal and directive tenet to which Baptist churches hold with great tenacity. This ideal has shined in the firmament of these free churches as the pole-star in the night sky. Yet as clear thinking reveals no such thing as the *individual* in society, neither can it discover the strictly *independent* church. With the rapid multiplication of churches there came the inevitable shading of the ideal.

They found it impossible to live, much less to grow, in isolation. Since each had so much in common with all the others they must associate themselves in order better to achieve Kingdom ends.

This movement away from the ideal toward ever-widening cooperation has been painful to many Baptists. To students of polity it has been most interesting. For therein they discover the struggle of a living organism to adapt itself to changing conditions. They witness a contest between the ideal and the practical, with the gradual ascendency of the latter. Differently stated, they see a constant search for some working formula for the churches which would at the same time safeguard the essential life of *the one* while associating with *the many* in cooperative enterprise. This conflict between the ideal and the real constitutes an arresting chapter in the growth of Baptist polity. In it is written the whole story of the rise of the Association; first for fellowship and inspiration, then for cooperative labors, generally of the missionary type. It records the birth and growth of Associations, City Mission Societies, State and National Conventions, the Baptist World Alliance, etc. (even a wide range of ecumenical interests), in and through which the churches activate " the Baptist World Mission." From the local church—conceived to be wholly independent—to the complex polity of today is a long journey. Baptist churches have been three hundred and fifty years covering that distance, and at the end find no essential loss in the virility of their principle of independency, but great gain in effectiveness as they forward Kingdom interests. Today agreement is general that the world-wide enterprises which the churches have in hand could not be carried forward without consistent and conscientious cooperation.

# The Baptist Doctrine of Church

Democracy and independency are the two chief planks in the platform of Baptist polity. As planks they have been something not merely to be stood upon, but timbers to be built into a high stockade safeguarding the members of the churches against ravenous wolves, so to speak, that wound and kill free souls. When soul liberty is thus guaranteed, say the Baptist folk, the way is open and broad for large personal growth and assured Kingdom progress. When each, enriched and strengthened by fellow disciples, is free to work out his own faith, he will grow into tallness of stature; when each finds liberty to do his own thinking in company with others of open mind, he will venture to "think the thoughts of God after Him"; when each may freely search the Scriptures for himself, clarifying his findings by conversation with other free searchers, new light will continually break forth from the sacred pages; and when each without let or hindrance may walk, in all the ways in which he goes with the strong Son of God, he will mature in a majesty not unlike that which becomes such a companionship. Such strength will bend its back beneath the weight of the forward-moving kingdom of heaven, and will gather power from the task. In other words, Christians are grown largely, if not wholly, by participation in the work of Christ; democracy and independency are held to be most conducive to that participation. Under their dominion religion by proxy does not prosper, for they bid each one to hold it and operate it in his own name, assured that he will grow thereby into "wisdom and stature, and in favor with God and men."

One need not dig deep into this manner of thinking to disclose the purpose which drives a Baptist church and gives direction to its developing polity. The aim is to produce the individual Christian, tall, straight and clean as a Southern pine, with ability to throw himself into the cooperative labor of lifting the walls of the temple of God. As the strength of the pack resides in the individual wolf, so the strength of the church and the virility of the expanding Kingdom reside in the quality of the individual disciple of the Lord. Men strong in their allegiance to Christ and his manner of living make a church " mighty to reduce the strongholds of evil " and build the ramparts of righteousness. The chief business of a church is to grow such men, then organize and send them forth as good soldiers in the army of the just and righteous, the loving and holy God.

The purpose to build a " Church," spelled with a capital C, lies without the range of Baptist interest. Organization, procedure, program, polity, and the institution in general are only means to an end, and not an end in themselves. All such have only one charter for existence, namely, their ability to serve the growing disciple. Not one of these is sacrosanct in itself, but may borrow such glory if it greatly ministers to inspire and enrich those who hunger to walk in His way who is the Light of the World. By its fruit is any item of polity to be judged. So speaks the voice of a Baptist church.

As polity cannot claim to be an end in itself, neither can democracy or independency. These are creative ideals which have produced what we call Baptist polity. And as their fruit is not sacred, neither are they in themselves. They may claim such honor in proportion as their fruit blesses the lives of men. At most they are living ideals. Even those churches which have bound themselves thereto " with hoops of steel " can claim only approximate realization. That they have sought stedfastly

to actualize in practice what they proclaim in theory few
will care to deny. As human society in which the churches
live has grown increasingly complex in all its manifestations, so have the churches grown more complex in
polity. Such lies as a necessity in the very nature of the
aim of the churches, which, as we understand it, is to
break the bread of life to a needy world. To do this,
complexity must be matched by adequate complexity—
which means a more involved polity or method of acting.
But in this movement, be it noted, the structural sim-
plicities of pure democracy and complete independency
have been supplemented by more involved items of polity.
Some are inclined to slur these creations as " machinery,"
or " overhead machinery." As a matter of fact, however, they are but further adaptations of living churches
to new conditions and demands. The figure of machinery
is not pertinent; an organism acquires new ways of
behavior but does not build machinery. These new ways
of acting now in our thought are but new items of polity,
and as such have come into being as has all the rest of
polity.

New ways may be more involved than previous ways,
but they must be tested by the ancient test, " By their
fruits." They are neither good nor bad ways *per se*.
Neither age nor youth in an item of polity is a guarantee
of its right to permanency. Only as these tend to make
more swift the feet of them who run therein as promoters of the King's business, are they ways worthy of
the churches. These runners impart to polity the spirit
and life of Him whom they serve, if they find the polity
worthy. Polity takes on the color and tone of that worthy
to be cherished when it continues to bless the runner and
hasten the day when Christ shall come into the fulness of

his own estate in the hearts of men. Any polity that does those two things is good, and may claim the blessing of God.

In conclusion, we indicate a significant corollary to the doctrine of soul liberty. Those who claim it for themselves must freely grant it to others. If in the exercise of their competency they have produced a polity for *their* churches, they must grant the like right to all others. Baptists have not been slow to recognize this implicate of their position, hence have no quarrel with those whose polity differs from their own. Neither are they of a mind to claim a higher degree of divine guidance in the working out of their polity. They do hold that the elements of democracy and independency predominate in the incipient polity of the New Testament churches. They abide stedfast in their conviction that these principles hold more possibilities for guiding the growth of competent souls into the life and ministry of Christ than any others discoverable in Scripture, or found in the church life of the centuries since. Hence each recurring generation of Baptists dedicates itself to the task of working out a polity of democracy and independency for its own day. Changes in details do not disturb since they are known to be inevitable. In the life-span of many now living practically all of the churches—at least in the North—have shifted from a close communion to an open communion polity; and the present day is said to be witnessing a steady movement toward so-called " open membership," or the practice of receiving *ad eundem* those who come from non-immersing churches. So far as one who lives near or in the midst of such changes may judge there is no apparent loss in either democracy or independency; competency seems equally well guarded under either the old or the new polity. Those who promote these changes claim for them a manifestation of a widening good-will and fraternity among the varying groups of Christians. If this is true the changes will doubtless prove to be justified, and will claim the benediction of the coming years.

### Topics for Group Discussion

1. Are doctrine and polity closely related in all branches of the Christian church? Let the group give illustrations. Which takes temporal precedence, doctrine or polity?

2. Is the doctrine of competency well grounded, and therefore destined to endure?

3. Tabulate the points of weakness and of strength in this doctrine, as it works itself out in the lives of people and their churches.

4. Is efficiency on the side of a democratic, or of a monarchial polity? Are Baptist churches as efficient as the Episcopal, for instance?

5. How can surrender to Christ be thought logical in a competent soul?

6. What are the main planks in the platform of Baptist polity? Indicate others that occur to the group.

### Books Worth Consulting

Leavenworth, Lynn, ed., *Great Themes in Theology.* The Judson Press, Philadelphia, 1958.

Lumpkin, William L., *Baptist Confessions of Faith.* The Judson Press, Philadelphia, 1959.

McCall, Duke K., ed., *What Is the Church? A Symposium of Baptist Thought.* The Broadman Press, Nashville, 1958.

# Polity and Practice in Baptist Churches

New Testament.

Robinson, William, *The Biblical Doctrine of the Church.* The Bethany Press, St. Louis, 1955.

Strong, Augustus Hopkins, *Systematic Theology.* The Judson Press, Philadelphia, 1907.

### PRACTICAL SUGGESTIONS

1. Make this chapter of practical value by leading the group to a study of their own church to discover to what extent the Baptist doctrine of competency is at work in its organizational life. It will be useful to see if it makes for unity or disunity; for a spirit of cooperation, or for so-called "rugged individualism." Particular attention may be directed to ascertaining whether or not the doctrine begets a personal responsibility proportionate to the liberty proclaimed; remembering that rights and duties always balance each other. Such a study should be fruitful in a deepened concern that the polity under which the church is operating be shaped so as to safeguard the widest possible soul-freedom consistent with necessary cooperation both within and beyond the local parish.

2. The leader might with profit make a study of the larger phases of denominational life, in order to determine the degree of respect given this basic doctrine of competency in actual practice. Does it aid, or retard, necessary cooperation in Kingdom affairs? Not long ago the writer read a paper on, "The Baptist Position," before a group of ministers. In the period of discussion the actual loyalty of this people to their own great, creative ideal was roundly challenged. Such terms as "uncooperative," "intolerant," "dogmatic," "creedal," "sacramental," and the like, were hurled about the room. What

are the facts? Surely, a recognition of soul-competency ought to beget a people broad of mind and generous of spirit. Not so?—unless perchance they are willing to sponsor the absurd position of the validity of competency for themselves only. It would be an interesting study to determine the degree of later-day loyalty to the principles of the fathers that called forth the Baptist people.

# III

## WORSHIP IN THE CHURCHES

Since "public preaching services" in Baptist churches are both significant and fixed in their program, it seems not inappropriate to consider them as a phase of polity. By our definition they are a phase of polity. These Sunday morning and evening services have generally been considered the chief ministry of the church. Institutional features, with comparatively few exceptions, have been held to be secondary; and by some, mere "frills" of the church's work. What these services do, or fail to do, for individuals, church, and community becomes, therefore, very important. They constitute the badge and banner of the churches, the obverse side of the shield with which they confront the world.

These services have been rather exclusively preaching services. They are set up and maintained for the proclamation of the gospel—as understood by each respective minister and church, of course! Churches composed of "competent" men and women, and ministered to by a preacher considered both "competent" and free, will feel themselves able to discover and herald the only true gospel of Christ. This has always provided the saving salt of variety in emphasis. Regarded as educational institutions, the churches have offered, therefore, a very broad curriculum. Emphases have ranged from the didactic, through the narrowly evangelistic, into the world-wide social and missionary outreach. Where these varying emphases have been maintained in a wise balance the people have been well instructed, and perhaps edified. When such balance has been lacking the outcome has been a narrow, single-track group, apt in developing a holier-than-thou attitude toward those not sharing their own bias.

The didactic emphasis has called out the finest ministry of the churches. Where the man in the pulpit has been preeminently the teacher, there have the people—granted his wisdom—been most built up and best directed in growing the abundant life. Such a pulpit has acquainted the people with the great doctrines of the church and their outreach into the life of individuals and society. They have come by such a ministry to see our Lord Jesus Christ in the majestic Figure of prophet, priest, teacher, and Saviour of men; by virtue of whose strength and beauty they are called to

> ". . . follow Him through heaven and hell,
> The earth, the sea, and the air!"

And so to have taught, "in all the ways of God and men," as to secure that sort of self-commitment to Christ as Lord of life, has served to give a crown of glory to the didactic ministry. Let it be written, Blessed are those men who have stood in their pulpits, year after year, to instruct the people in all the wisdom and love of God, for verily they shall be known as builders of the kingdom of heaven.

A second emphasis in a well-balanced ministry, by and through the preaching services of the Baptist churches, is that of sounding the evangel, of proclaiming the glad news of salvation in Christ. This emphasis has characterized the Baptist people as those with an evangelistic passion and is chief among the causes of their notable increase in numbers. Where the fires of this passion are either banked or put out one can scarcely recognize a church as being of the Baptist order; at any rate, something is missing from it that history leads one to expect.

Increasingly this " zeal for souls "—as the old-time preachers put it—is finding expression through the educational processes of the well-organized and wisely directed church. It aims at the same goal as the older evangelism: self-commitment to Jesus Christ and the manner of living to which he calls. But unlike that, it assumes that the wise course is to root the new life in sound religious education, so that it may come to full flower by a natural rather than a forced process. This method is certain to have increasing vogue in the churches because it calls for careful nurture from the very cradle, and gives promise of finer fruitage when the young person chooses to espouse and follow his Lord. To this end it is essential that religious education keep individual self-commitment and continuing growth in Christ thereafter as its milepost and goal, respectively.

Essential as the evangelistic emphasis is, its too exclusive emphasis has in some sections come near converting a good into an evil. It has brought the saving of souls into disrepute, made the noble work of soulwinning a laughing matter. So-called campaigns have been accompanied by something akin to ballyhoo, which has caused the religiously sensitive and refined to turn away, sick at heart. The accompanying noise and bluster, and the type of minister they have too frequently called to the fore, have all conspired against the finer things of the spirit. Happily, most Baptist churches are now turning their backs upon this cheap and blasphemous " show," and are seeking to recover the sane evangelistic note that in former times was theirs; and to sound it in such quality of tone as to give hope for the capturing of this generation for Christ.

The social emphasis, which includes the missionary, has greatly enriched the ministry of the churches. It has taken the church-membership outside itself, given it a centrifugal urge toward society and the larger world. This emphasis has blessed the churches not less than the world. Some forty years ago Johanna Pirscher wrote a little volume, *Growth Without End,* whose significant philosophy held that a life ceased to grow only when it ceased to have a living investment in others and turned in upon itself. That thesis has found vindication in the missionary Baptist churches, and in all churches that have desired to share, to serve and to minister. These churches have renewed their youth with the passing years; have found themselves powerful factors in the creation of a Christian public opinion; and have entered upon a ministry of health and healing to the spiritually poor and sick.

Baptist history teaches plainly that the churches bearing this name have been apt in teaching, gifted in winning to discipleship, and zealous in social outreach. It indicates that those churches have weighed most in Kingdom influence which have maintained these three features in a well-rounded ministry. But in all that history one seeks in vain to discover a positive note on the worship of God. To assume therefrom that these people have never worshiped in sincerity would be grossly unfair, not to say untrue. However, that silence regarding worship is tremendously significant; it means that Baptists have not only not majored in worship, but that they have given little attention thereto. Other emphases, good and noble, have been consistently maintained; and these we have noted. But worship itself has never been an emphasis in the program of the Baptist churches; an omission that constitutes, we think, a very sad lack. Let us pursue this matter further.

Public services, as noted above, have been for preaching. The people have ever been called to their meeting-places to listen to sermons. They came to be instructed, to hear the challenge of the evangel, or to catch a vision of fields afar, "white unto the harvest." Wisely instructed, they learned much about God; evangelized, they knew the experience of regeneration through the grace of Christ; and made sensitive in conscience concerning the ills and needs of men everywhere, each enlarged within his own heart the borders of the kingdom of heaven. All this is commendable. The fact remains, however, that the people have been accustomed to go to church to hear the preacher rather than to hear God, to wait upon the preacher rather than upon God.

In practical results this, not overemphasis, but too exclusive emphasis on preaching has not been altogether salutary, either for pew or pulpit. It has tended to make the one hypercritical and the other the purveyor of honeyed words. Naturally so, when the hearing of preaching is considered the supreme religious exercise of the pew, and ability to please the hearer the high standard of judgment for the clergy. But what is more to the point, not to say baneful, is the fact that in this preaching-hearing process it is possible to leave God out of any great consideration—possible, and even actually so. A distinguished preacher of the past generation was a visitor at the theological seminary where the writer was a student. In the course of an address he gave young ministers this touchstone of success: "Find out what the people want, and then give that to them." Verily! that is exactly the way for the Christian ministry to lose its soul and the pew its capacity to hear the voice of God in his prophet. But it is a logical outcome of neglecting the first and major reason for church-going.

And that superlative reason? None other than this, namely, that men might in some life-changing sense see God; feel him near, hear him speak, wait upon him; for "They that wait upon the Lord shall renew their strength"; and nowhere is it written, "They that wait upon preaching shall renew their strength." As a matter of fact, they often are not renewed—as every modest preacher admits and the pew knows, to its sorrow. Theodore Roosevelt was wiser than most of us, as indicated by his writing that he was, at certain seasons, a regular attendant at a little church, ministered to by a good but not great man, because there in quiet and reverent surroundings he was able to commune with God. Many Baptists, on the contrary, would simply have been bored. The sermon's being mediocre would have spoiled it all. Yet a great statesman in those same circumstances found God! Those "many Baptists" have a highly developed taste for sermons; Mr. Roosevelt had a soul trained to sense the presence of the divine.

To be sure, in the non-liturgical churches, Baptist included, the pulpit talks about God, and ventures even to speak for God; but therein lies a subtle snare, a temptation to convince that men may gain God and godliness merely by talk. Religion by talk! The world is sick unto death of such. And moreover, "The highest cannot be spoken." The Eternal must be sensed, felt, heard; like a footfall in the silence at close of day. "They that wait upon the Lord . . ."; but alas! how little "waiting" in the average preaching service! The ideal is to keep things on the hum, with never a pause or moment of silence. A service that does not move right on from invocation to benediction is considered dull and uninteresting. The preacher unable to conduct a service full of movement and dash is generally considered too slow—and will be sent to the human discard without much ceremony. To " wait upon the Lord " is a prophetic injunction that means nothing to those schooled in church-going that they may " hear the sermon."

There came over into early Christianity from the older faith two distinct strains, that of the temple and that of the synagogue. The temple was a house of God, a place of worship; the synagogue, a place of instruction. In the one men were asked to come up for direct dealings with Jehovah, the Lord of Hosts; in the latter they assembled to hear the law expounded. The history of the Christian movement across all the intervening centuries lays bare these two living, creative strains. At times they are skilfully woven into a fabric of rich pattern, and then again each separates itself and takes its own way as though the other did not exist. The temple, or worship strain, alone, has produced here and there an elaborate ritualism in whose intricacies the common man has become lost, mired in a bog of superstition. His soul cries out for instruction; but there is no one to heed his cry. The synagogue strain has likewise separated itself and, alone, has converted a place of worship into a classroom where men are instructed *about God*. Either of these when unaccompanied by the other never fails to eventuate in sterility. Each strain needs the other, now to check, now to enrich.

Preaching churches are essentially Christian synagogues; they are places of instruction. Their function is didactic. They need the corrective of the temple strain. Instruction needs to be empowered by the practice of conscious worship; and worship needs instruction to save it from a barren formalism. To separate the two sides of a shield is to destroy it. To divorce the didactic from the worshipful is a like folly.

The truth of this contention has been coming to the Baptist and other non-liturgical churches with telling results within the last two decades. There is a worship movement abroad among them. Its force is sufficient to change completely old "auditoriums"—places for listening—into houses for worship, and to give us new church buildings dominated by the worship interest and motif. It is moving the church furniture about, placing at the center the communion-table, the symbol of the mysterious Presence. It is moving minister and Bible to either side, thus indicating that in the presence of the Divine these take a secondary place. God, and not the preacher, is coming to occupy the place of focal interest and attention. Public services are taking on a new quietness, reverence, and dignity, the people gathering as questers after the Eternal. Yet they have not come to despise preaching. On the contrary, they are setting the sermon in a worship atmosphere, as a jewel in the ring. As the worship passion is fed, people will demand better preaching; preaching fit to instruct souls aflame, after the great adventure of having struck hands with the heavenly Father.

The worship movement, coming into our churches like a tidal wave, is compelling a change in the structural polity of public services. It demands that they be recast, leaving behind the features of the common public assembly and bringing in the artistry befitting a place where men gather before the God and Father of them all. Whither this demand will drive it is too early to predict, but that it calls for revolutionary changes no one can doubt who senses at all its significance. In the formative, creative years ahead church leaders must be taught by history—whose admonition is that instruction and worship be maintained in a wise balance; that temple and synagogue strains be woven with skill into the pattern of enriched public religious assemblies.

Note what lopsided emphases do to the minister. When the didactic is in such ascendency as to eclipse all else, he takes the place at the center and proceeds at once to exploit himself in the interests of what he teaches. If by roaring like a lion or standing on the pulpit he can gain attention for his message, he may engage in just those antics. He thereby makes himself an " interesting " person, with an equally interesting lesson to teach. And because his activist methods get results, he may possibly be pardoned therefor. At any rate, the didactic, synagogue strain has often been captured by the boisterous and clownish whose doings in the pulpit do little credit to Christ and his church. On the other hand, when the worship motif has wholly set aside the work of instruction the results not infrequently have been quite as disastrous. In such case the minister tends to become the shrinking, sandal-shod priest who goes perfunctorily through some elaborate ritual, chanting or mumbling unintelligible phrases and nothings.

Between these two extremes is the golden mean that gives balance and poise to the church's public services, and spiritual health to the minister. In such a position he identifies himself in thought with his people and becomes the one who goes before them, leading up into the presence of God, whom they together worship. It is no longer a case of teacher and taught, but instead a silent, worshiping group under the leadership of one who has learned well the chaste and holy way that leads mortal men before the Eternal. Such high adventure of soul does something beyond estimate to the minister. For one thing, it will give him, in exchange for his filthy rags of platform technique, a royal robe of dignity and modesty, and for the period of instruction—the sermon should be instructive—a weight of authority before unknown to his teaching ministry. In time this may be fulfilled in him: a minister with fulness of stature, who exemplifies at once priest, prophet, and teacher; the good minister of the Lord Jesus Christ, apt in being all things to all men.

There are those who are fearful that the present-day worship movement will enventuate in religious and moral prettiness. They fear that men and women will go to church, enjoy a "lovely service," be given a feast of the beautiful and thereafter return to their homes self-satisfied and willing to let it all end there. If that fear be well-founded, then what a tragedy is sweeping like a tide into our churches! And let it be written that religious history does give some reason for such a fear. Repeatedly that which we have called the temple strain has issued in complexity of ritual and empty formalism; it has centered attention upon the frills of the hothouse and forgotten all about the flowers that should be growing there. Such formalisms often breed religious lassitude, divorce religion and morality, and divert organized religion from its deeper, healing and life-giving channels. Indeed, history does give cause for such fear; hence we may not despise him who sounds the alarm at this hour.

The person who is thus alarmed is not likely to be calmed by one who lays before him the equally disastrous results of a long time overemphasis on the synagogue or didactic strain. If the temple strain has left the church impotent in formalisms, the other has talked the church to death. Contemporaneous Christianity is not notably vital and electric with the crusading passion; but it is *much instructed*. The people of the churches *know,* they are filled to the brim with doctrines, they know by heart the organizational set-up of their respective denominations—and yet there is an appalling lack of that devotion which emerges in terms of power.

It is this situation that gives dynamic to the present-day worship emphasis; men and women are seeking to fill life's emptiness by contacting the resources of power which they believe to be in God, the Father of our Lord Jesus Christ and of us all. Such a day calls for an understanding guide in the parish minister. He must be one acquainted with highways that have hitherto led to dead-ends, and avoid them; one who fears overemphases of whatsoever nature. As for the matters of worship and teaching, he will wed them so that they may mutually strengthen each other and correct each other, to the end that together they may richly minister to men. Under guidance of such ministers he who is alarmed about liturgical developments will gather a new confidence when he witnesses great preaching that fires those who worship with a moral passion to seek the Kingdom and the righteousness of God in all the ways of life. Likewise, one who sees the current religious poverty—the fruit of religion-by-talk—will take new heart, knowing that now a wiser ministry is dedicated to the high calling of leading men to seek vital, life-empowering relations with the

Eternal. In brief, contemporaneous Christianity will regain its soul if it can once more make men God-conscious by and through the worship experience; and then persistently and passionately instruct them in all the ways of God for men. The worship experience plows and harrows the soil of the soul into which wise instruction drops the seed of eternal life. Both plowing and sowing are necessary if rationally a harvest is to be expected. Either without the other ends in fruitlessness.

The worship emphasis demands change in the polity of public services for Baptist churches. The structural framework must be enlarged so as to support worship as well as instruction, so as to make way for the presence of God as well as that of the instructor. It must be ordered in accord with a new artistry capable of tempting the souls of men upward toward the Infinite; for worship is the finest art known to mortals.

While polity as such deals with mechanics, it may yet be mechanics plus. A certain engine runs in oil; it is an engine plus. There is a needed change that will immerse the polity of certain public services in the atmosphere of worship. This atmosphere is compounded of quiet and beauty, begetting reverence and humility of spirit. As the skeleton hides itself beneath living flesh, so must polity retire to the shadows behind that atmosphere which is a "call to worship" for everyone who enters the church portals. Though hidden, it must give sustaining strength to orderliness of procedure and to a studied purpose in every act of the hour. Baptist services have often been "without form and void." Certain things were to be done, such as reading of the Scriptures and singing of hymns, but just when or how was of no particular concern. The worship hunger makes such careless informalities impossible because they irritate the finer sensibilities; and hence negate worship.

An order of worship is a requirement. It constitutes a highway, studiously laid out by the minister, who, having himself found God in that direction, has widened his own beaten trail for his people. In such a program historic elements will be employed—music, silence, Scripture, prayer, the offering—but placed in such sequence as to have meaning for the worshipers and in such relation one to the other as to advance the people in their quest. An order of worship has the virtue, moreover, of inspiring the gathering-up of loose ends, of eliminating extraneous details, and of introducing orderliness into the service; in themselves no small gains. Certainly Baptist polity can stand the strain of these changes; necessary, if things are "to be done in decency and in order"— as conceived by those increasing multitudes whose cultural good taste cannot be ignored, much less outraged by crass and bungling informalities.

We turn to the mechanics of an order of worship with the definite conviction, however, that such a thing has value only as it aids the worshiping group. As a trellis is good just so long as it serves the rose that climbs over it, so is the order of worship a valid instrument to that degree in which it helps those who worship to ascend into the presence of the Lord.

## AN ORDER OF WORSHIP

PRELUDE.
CALL TO WORSHIP—Response.
INVOCATION.
CHORAL SELECTION (or hymn sung by the people).
READING OF THE SCRIPTURES.
HYMN.

PASTORAL PRAYER.
OFFERING.
ORGAN MEDITATION (or period of silence).
SERMON.
PRAYER AND BENEDICTION.
PERIOD OF QUIET, FOR MEDITATION.
POSTLUDE.

Such a program as the above may either spring into living significance or remain wooden and dead. Let us move it into a house really dedicated to divine worship and there undertake to breathe into it the breath of life.

*Prelude.* The people are assembling. It is our desire that immediately they be inducted into an atmosphere conducive to worship; that their spirits be quieted, and brought into harmony with the purpose of this hour; that their thoughts be turned toward God and godly living. Nothing is more effective in creating this atmosphere of worship than noble music, played quietly by skilled and reverent hands. The organ, that churchly instrument par excellence, is highly preferable, though the piano is a fair substitute when the other is not available. When Prelude is matched by quiet and reverence on the part of the people, all will be electric and expectant as the minister enters, to be the leader of a company who are assembled ready for the worship adventure.

*Call to Worship.* At this moment, when all are alert and attentive, their leader enters, serves notice by his bearing that he fully senses the significance of this hour, and calls upon the waiting people to begin their advance up to " the hill of the Lord." The words he shall employ in his Call, whether or not people or choir, or both, shall respond, are details that may be left to the good taste and understanding heart of the minister. We personally like some antiphonal arrangement. In such case one or the other may suggest, "Let us sing unto the Lord, our God," thus making the "Praise God," "All Hail," or some other well-chosen outburst of praise both appropriate and natural.

*Invocation.* This element in the Order assumes that now the group is approaching the living God, who is reverently addressed on their behalf by their leader in the Invocation. The divine blessing is invoked upon these now advancing who are devoutly seeking God's face. If it be desired to elaborate the service at this point, it would be appropriate and psychologically sound for the Invocation to be preceded by the recital of some statement of faith (addressed to God, before whom the people stand), and followed by a devout Amen by choir, or by the congregation.

*Choral Selection.* From the Call to Worship the people have been standing. Let them now be seated in quiet, attentive attitude. Here is the opportunity for the choir. It may do one of two things, either speak to God on behalf of the people, or speak to the people on behalf of God. Which, should have been carefully determined in advance and in the light of the worship theme for the hour. If the choir does the former, then in thought it identifies itself with the people, stands *among the people,* as it were, and on their behalf sings unto Him whom they worship. If, on the contrary, it sings some word of the Lord to the people, then it stands apart while delivering His message.

*Reading the Scripture.* Like the Choral Selection the portion of the Scriptures chosen for reading may be either a message from God to men (e. g., Isa. 42:6-9) or a cry of men to God (e. g., Ps. 74). In the one case the people sit as those who hear, while in the other each worshiper voices the deeps of his own soul by means of the Word being read. In whichever direction the reading moves, it should be read with a reverent impressivenes befitting the occasion. For careless reading of the Bible in public worship there can be only condemnation. If, for instance, the passage be one in which God speaks, then the reader is under bond so to read as to make the congregation hear God. It is no time or place for the mumbling of words, as though they were without meaning. In addition to proper reading, so important is this element of Scripture in an Order of Service that it may well be preceded by a petition of the people, like " Break Thou the Bread of Life," or, " O Word of God Incarnate." One stanza of such a hymn, sung quietly and unannounced, by a people seated and expectant will enhance the ministry of the Word. The reading may well be followed by a fitting response, by the choir or congregation, or both.

*Hymn.* Here the people express themselves in song. The Order has thus far led them into God's presence, and through choral and scriptural messages, let us say, they have heard God speak to them. Now they are to speak to him in reply. The hymn, therefore, must be carefully chosen, so that it will enable those who sing to say what they now wish to say and may appropriately say. If not carefully selected the result may be to violate the worship theme and hence negate the effects desired. The essential is that the hymn announced shall be a vehicle by means of which the worshipers are furthered in their quest for and communion with the Father.

*The Pastoral Prayer.* Where the hymn leaves the people, just there the minister, standing among the people, takes up their case in prayer. The pastoral prayer is not

E        [ 53 ]

his prayer, but the prayer of the people which he is elected and privileged to voice. On their behalf he comes, their advocate before the throne. Here it is that the minister, in our opinion, reaches the zenith of his priestly function. If so, this prayer issues to him a superlative challenge therein to be at his best in devotional mood, his choicest in language, his noblest in thought and his most reverent in general bearing. Anything less than the finest of which he is capable is blameworthy, if not blasphemous.

*The Offering.* The offering, properly understood and properly integrated as a unit in the Order, should be a climax in the worship experience. Having ascended into divine presence, having voiced his deepest life through the foregoing exercises, the worshiper now comes to the moment of personal dedication. His offering is a symbol of that dedication. With his gift he is saying, " By and through this, my God and Father, I lay my life before thee ; do with it as thou wilt."

Since the offering should be made thus climactic, it is incumbent upon the leader of worship to see that it is presented and received in an atmosphere befitting its significance. Good music is appropriate. A quiet dignity and reverence on the part of all are positively essential. Impassioned pleas and ballyhoo of every sort are to be considered anathema at this point of the program, where men and women come before God to present their gifts and their lives.

*The Sermon.* Let us assume that a certain worshiper has said in his heart, " O God, I am a sinful man ; grant me thy forgiveness. I shall seek henceforth to live the good life, even as it was in Christ Jesus, to whom I give full allegiance." Then follows the sermon, which instructs this worshiper regarding the good life upon which he has resolved, and inspires him for the task of carrying through to success. It may be said that the service up to this point has been plowing, harrowing, and generally preparing the soil of the man's inner life. Now comes the minister's great opportunity to sow therein the precious seed of the gospel of God and his beloved Son. The call is for superlative preaching; preaching with an excellence worthy of one who has just been in life-changing communion with the Lord of all the earth. The worship emphasis in contemporaneous church-life is crying aloud for a quality of preaching unexcelled by that of any age, however great its preaching.

*The Conclusion* of the service may vary; it is only required that it come to an end with an impressiveness in harmony with all that has gone before. The people should go away in the full glow of their worship experience, and the undiminished urge to the good life given by the sermon. Our thought is that a period of silence is unexcelled for the closing. Most Baptist congregations are in need of an occasional silence in which to meditate, to hear God speak. Let the service close on the high pitch of an electric silence, ended by a noble choral "Amen."

A people who believe themselves "competent" in all matters religious will hold themselves competent truly to worship as has been commanded, "Thou shalt worship the Lord thy God." Moreover, they will not doubt the right invested in that same competency to order such changes in polity and procedure as are required to make way for a worship emphasis in the public services of the churches.

## Polity and Practice in Baptist Churches

### Topics for Group Discussion

1. What should be the primary aim of the man who goes to church?

2. What do you understand by worship? What is the desired objective of a Service of Worship?

3. Trace temple and synagogue strains in the various Christian denominations and sects, evaluating each such strain.

4. What have been the characteristic emphases in the life and work of the Baptist churches? Have these together constituted a well-balanced program?

5. Contrast the conceptions of the minister as preacher, and the minister as leader of the people in their hours of public worship.

6. What dangers do you apprehend in liturgical or worship developments? How may public worship be safeguarded against these?

7. Discuss the meaning of the offering in a well-integrated, or unified, Order of Service, suggesting ways for making it more meaningful.

### Books Worth Consulting

Maxwell, W. D., *Outline of Christian Worship; Its Development and Forms.* Oxford University Press, New York, 1940.

Otto, Rudolph (translated by J. W. Harvey), *The Idea of the Holy.* Oxford University Press, New York, 2nd edition, 1950.

Wise, B. Fred, ed., *Christian Worship, A Hymnal.* The Judson Press, Philadelphia, 1955.

# Worship in the Churches

## PRACTICAL SUGGESTIONS

1. Ask each member of the group to prepare an Order of Worship capable of being used in his own church. On the basis of these let the group work together to create an Order enriched by group thought. Would your minister install this Order for a few months in your church?

2. Make it a group project to collect calendars from many churches of various denominations, with a view to the study of the Orders of Worship printed therein.

## IV

## THE WITNESS OF HISTORY

History is always an adequate check on revelation, even on a revealed polity. When history vindicates, men have more respect for that which is revealed. Every institution, every human cause, every idea asks naught save the vindication of time, the eternal sifter of gold from dross.

The Baptist churches may now appeal to history, the history of some twelve generations, for its witness to the practicability of their polity. If the pragmatic test is valid in relation to the discovery of the will of God, or in so far as it is valid, Baptist polity has divine sanction. At any rate this polity has " worked " to the satisfaction of an increasing host of people, and by that token seems to attain the approval of the great Head of the church.

Baptists, as we now know them, had their beginning very early in the seventeenth century, in England and Holland. They came heralding soul competency and full religious liberty. It was under the banner of soul-freedom that they marched across the intervening centuries down to the present. In numbers and influence their growth has been phenomenal; from a mere handful of " regenerate, baptized believers," their membership has increased to more than twenty millions, and from a despised band of heretics, they have come to an honored place among the Christian peoples of the world.

As all know, the Baptist family stock is English. Taking its rise in England this family has sent its children into many lands, colonizers for Christ and freedom. Despite this modern dispersion among the nations and islands of the sea, sturdiness, vision and virtue have characterized also those who remained at home. A minority group, not infrequently sinned against, and consistently unaided by the Established Church, they have nevertheless succeeded in making a leavening contribution to the total religious thought and life of the British Isles, out of all proportion to their numbers.

The world in which English Baptists have lived and wrought has been manifestly a world quite different from that in which American and Canadian Baptists have come to maturity. In the one case there was an old and ordered society, in the other the new-born, the pioneering, the fashioning of that which was to be. It is not surprising, therefore, that some differences in method of manifesting the life of the churches has arisen, some variation in practices and polity. The surprise is that we find so little variation. That little variation, moreover, is in non-essentials. In soul competency and freedom, in guidance by the Scriptures, and in exaltation of Christ as Lord of life and the Church's High Priest, they are one. From the days of John Bunyan to the present English Baptists have fellowshiped so-called " mixed membership " churches and have held in high honor such advocates thereof as Doctors Robert Hall (1761-1831) and John Clifford (1836-1923). *The Baptist Handbook* as early as 1901 listed thirty-four such churches. This mixed membership practice is the most notable variation that has developed during these three hundred and fifty years; and that variation is passing, since in recent years a large number of American Baptist churches have adopted the " open membership " polity.

## *Polity and Practice in Baptist Churches*

Baptist leaven reached these Western shores with Roger Williams in 1631; a leaven too potent to remain quiescent. Williams came as one who seeks a haven of religious liberty, but soon discovered that the Puritans of the Boston Bay Colony were sponsors of a brand of soul-freedom that gave generous guarantees only to those who agreed with them, and not to those who were in disagreement. Williams arrived in Boston inoculated with the separation-of-church-and-state germ. Under the heat of controversy the germ became decidedly active. The Puritan theocracy was soon the object of his open attack, with the result that he was compelled to flee Boston, and then take refuge, in midwinter, with the Indians in the wilds to the west and south of that colony. The next spring he emerged on the warmer waters of Narragansett Bay, where he established the Providence Plantation, the first state in human history to guarantee to all absolute religious liberty.

Baptists have ground for their belief that this incident was under divine guidance. The trade winds of freedom were blowing across seas and continents and the atmosphere of the New World was electric with the hopes and ideals of human liberty. At such an hour God directed Roger Williams to plant in this fertile soil a seed like that of mustard. It has grown into a mighty tree. The Baptist tenet of soul liberty found its way into the Constitution of the United States, denying to Congress the power to make any law respecting religion. Thus separation of church and state—the principle for enunciating which Roger Williams fled to the refuge of friendly Indians—became a creative influence in the whole religious life of America.

From the beginning Baptists have been of the common

people; the kind of people who generally have been the oppressed and the exploited; common people who were hungry, therefore, not only for release, but for their own equal " place in the sun." The dynamic doctrine of soul competency in all matters of religion, with its long reach into realms other than the religious, was peculiarly congenial to such folks. It came to them as the Magna Charta of their rights and liberties, and of course they seized it and hugged it to their bosoms.

This fact looms large in explanation of the numerical growth of Baptists in the great republic of the Western world. Competency of soul and the time-spirit were wed, as though created for each other. Men and women who were competent as high priests of their own souls would conceive themselves equally competent to conquer the wilderness and lay deep the foundations of the state. And so it has been; these Baptists drove westward, a sturdy portion of the pioneering vanguard; they helped to subdue every mile of the receding frontier, and participated in building the mighty empire of the West. Wherever they went—and they went everywhere—they lived by and preached their great idea of competency, together with its manifold corollaries for private life and public service. Hence East and West, North and South, are all alike dotted with thousands of Baptist churches that are living by their basic tenets of liberty and freedom in Christ.

The issue of human slavery in the United States produced among its regrettable fruits a division of the Baptist family into Northern and Southern. In May, 1814, Baptists of all sections had united to form " The General Convention of the Baptist Denomination in the United States for Foreign Missions." This body, meeting every third year, came to be popularly known—though unofficially—as " The Triennial Convention." It functioned effectively until 1845. In the meeting of 1844 the slavery issue flared up with violent heat; however, the crisis seemed to have been met and passed in this resolution:

*Resolved,* That in cooperating together as members in this Convention in the work of foreign missions, we disclaim all sanctions either expressed or implied, whether of slavery or antislavery; but as individuals we are free to express and to promote elsewhere our views on these subjects in a Christian manner and spirit.

Despite this conciliatory resolution a post-Convention statement of policy was practically forced from the executive board:

If anyone who should offer himself for a missionary, having slaves, should insist on retaining them as his property, we could not appoint him. One thing is certain, we can never be a party to an arrangement which would imply approbation of slavery.

This announced policy, seemingly not called for by the dictates of wisdom, led directly to the formation of the Southern Baptist Convention in the following year, 1845.

Many years have passed since that fateful day; eleven decades in which Baptists North and South have developed each their own world-wide work for advancing the cause of their common Lord. Greatly indeed have both been prospered by the blessing of the Father who pays little public heed to the passions and hatreds, heats and divisions, of his children. Numbers have multiplied beyond belief, the churches enrolling even millions of adult communicants. Moreover, into their hands have come vast holdings in property and endowments, held in trust for the forwarding of the Kingdom enterprise. In the meantime a generation has come which has no personal remembrance of the war between the States, and which feels increasing embarrassment because of the house divided against itself. Meanwhile they press forward on many fronts the Master's cause in the earth. Despite unfortunate divisions, all are Baptists, maintaining a remarkable unity of life and polity.

That such a people, people of the common lot, should essay to build schools and colleges would ordinarily seem unexpected. Such high endeavor might better be left to those of learning, position and wealth. But not so; men endowed by God with religious competency are surely competent also to found schools for their children. As a result, no people in America have made a richer and profounder contribution to the educational life of the nation than have the Baptists. What power there is in a single, creative idea!

Let us be reminded that our word about Baptist polity is, that throughout these centuries of growth—varied and manifold though it was—the simple, democratic polity has been adequate. This is history's vindication. All that any people may legitimately ask of the polity of their churches is that it prove equal to the task of an ever-widening ministry to the world. There is nothing sacred about any polity; it is a means of getting things done effectively, " in decency and in order." What Baptists claim and all they claim is that their polity has done that fairly well. Among its glories has been its ability readily to change in order to meet changing needs. New Testament polity shone with this identical glory.

Increasing numbers—for, as noted, Baptists have increased remarkably—put a considerable strain upon any polity, especially a democratic polity. The New England town-meeting, a pure democracy, is admirably effective in the small community, but would be hopelessly ineffective in a large community like Boston, and much more so in the Commonwealth of Massachusetts. And when to numbers there is added an increasing general knowledge, the strain on pure democracy becomes all the greater. The demand for the most effective means of getting the work of the Kingdom done becomes more insistent at the same time that democracy is becoming unwieldly and inefficient. Baptists find themselves at that station today. Their problem is to safeguard competency and at the same time arrive at efficiency. We believe the democratic spirit will be equal to the need thus revealed.

Ours is another day when the tides of democracy are running high. Consequently, it may well be a new day of opportunity for Baptists. In such a time men find need for an interpretation of religion that can give reassurance of their competency—competency to meet the demands of the new freedoms which are involved in the self-determination of states, in an enlarged democratization of industry, in a more just distribution of the good things of life, in a larger leisure and in the call for a newer education, designed to relate young and old more directly to the task of living. At any rate, such an era of significant change as today engulfs us will hunger and thirst after the courage and fortitude of earlier pioneers. Just that is the need of the hour. The times cry out for men who, far from being mere drifters, and waiters for the return of better days, will rise up to fight and conquer; men who believe that under God they are wholly competent successfully to meet every crisis. The Baptist interpretation of Christianity, which so fortified the pioneer of yesterday, is desperately needed today.

# The Witness of History

Whether or not this liberty-loving people shall be able to serve well this generation depends wholly upon two considerations. First, will it major in soul-competency until every member of its churches conceives himself an ambassador of God adequately able to make a positive contribution to the soul of the time? and secondly, can the polity of Baptist churches endure the strain of this superlative task? It is more than certain that major emphasis upon peripheral matters on the one hand and standpattism on the other will block the needed achievment. A polity long characterized by an elasticity adequate to new demands, must today run fluid. Having reached a stage where democracy and independency may tend to become unwieldly and inefficient, there is challenge for an open-minded restudy of the entire polity side of Baptist denominational life. The general problem involved in this restudy is to find such a balance between the demands of individual competence and the necessities of wide and definite cooperation as shall make possible the reaching of the challenging goals conceived by denominational leaders of vision.

Close at hand is a pointed illustration, namely, where Baptists are confronted by the baffling problems of the great city. The cosmopolitan areas are examples of the most complex social structure, wherein the life of the people becomes wholly socialized. Each is dependent upon a hundred individuals and institutions; independence remains as a mere vestige. Cooperation to the minutest detail is the order that must be accepted, under penalty of death. Now in the midst of such a socialized order is planted an independent Baptist church. It may easily become a small island over which the social and civic tides roll, to destroy. Just this has happened in many cities. The churches, overemphasizing independency and self-sufficiency, have kept at their individual tasks until wholly submerged. The record of Baptists in our large cities is not glorious; they have possibly fared worse in these centers of massed population than any other major body of Christians. The reason is perfectly evident; the historic Baptist polity has failed at a crucial hour; the very hour when the people were in sore need of the witness of competency. Failure to exercise competency in creating such cooperative effort as would have enabled the churches to face the problems of the city with a united front, is not complimentary. By this manifest weakness they largely sinned away the days of opportunity in many of the greater cities. There is, however, yet time to retrieve in centers that are to be the great cities of tomorrow. As never before Baptist polity is today being tested; tested at the point of adaptability to meet new needs; an adaptability largely in terms of city-wide, state-wide, nation-wide, and even world-wide cooperation.

This is an age of cooperative effort, and since religion lives in this age, it is under bond to learn the cooperative techniques, or else forfeit its right to live. That most branches of the Christian church sense this is manifest to even a casual observer; the areas of cooperation between and among denominations widen year by year. Only the overcautious, the religiously self-righteous, or the patently stubborn, are not on the roll of honor. This day is ringing down the curtain on sectarianism of every sort; it has played its rôle, the applause has subsided, and the lights will soon be out. Baptists, sometimes converting competency into self-sufficient complacency by a strange alchemy of reasoning, are nevertheless among those who are forward in cooperations of many kinds. In local communities, in home and foreign missionary enterprises, in the National and World Councils of the Churches of Christ, to cite but a few instances, they are making peace with the " time spirit," and—let it be said—also with the heart of God.

Facing this challenge Baptists will be wise to bear constantly in mind a fair perspective, which sets polity in its right and proper relationships to message, major purpose, and life. Polity is that complex of method by means of which a certain message is heralded, through which major purposes are forwarded, and by the grace of which the lives of people are strengthened and enriched. Polity is tested by its effectiveness in producing desired fruit; failing in this, let it be digged about and given one more brief chance, and then boldly digged up, if barrenness continues.

Baptist history is not silent on the point of change. Independent churches early found it expedient to form Associations. By so doing they became the less independent. Every page of their history tells the same story, even down to the recent shift to open communion and the contemporaneous swing toward open membership. The voice of history speaks commendation for the polity of the Baptist churches, its strength being—as noted above—in its ready adaptability when confronted by new conditions and new opportunities.

In the light of three and a half centuries of history— in many respects notable history—Baptists may be pardoned for seeing God's blessing upon their movement; including their polity. In both their numbers and their influence they have reason to rejoice in the Lord. But they should not be pardoned if they saw divine approval of *their* polity alone. Other communions also have greatly prospered; for example, the Methodists, who, coming upon the scene later even than Baptists, have challenged them in numbers and in the outreach of a splendid ministry. Speaking of the churches in the large cities, one of the city missions statesmen among Baptists says that Episcopalian and Presbyterian churches are succeeding, while those of his denomination fail; they remain and minister, while his either die or retreat. The fact would seem to be, therefore, that the Lord blesses whatever polity gets his work done in the world with grace and effectiveness. It is a Baptist task to make Baptist polity worthy of God's continuing blessing.

The centuries during which Baptists have wrought have witnessed a continuous rising of the tide of democracy. This seems to have come "in the fulness of time," or "for such a day as this." At least the times have been propitious for the development of the free and democratic in the field of religion. For the doctrine of liberty and fraternity, heralded by political units, Baptists have provided the religious counterpart in their doctrine of the competency of the human personality; and this they have institutionalized in a host of churches whose structural lines constitute a democratic polity. Now if history has actually vindicated Baptists and their free spirit in religion, their influence should be seen to be effective in changing other religious groups and the polity of their churches. Even the ordinary observer must admit that there has been a very decided drift toward democratization of procedure—that is, in polity—in every one of the other denominations; that even the so-called state churches are far less dominated by the state than formerly. The drift has been decidedly in the direction of the positions of freedom early taken by Baptists. How much credit for this drift this pioneering group may claim, and how much is due to the time-spirit, we shall not attempt to say. Doubtless the strands of influence which have been weaving the pattern of freedom, which because of early espousal may be called the Baptist pattern, set up in democratic polity, constitute a tangled skein. We shall leave to others the nice task of untangling. In the meantime Baptists may be permitted to discover continuing vindication of their life and ministry in the above-mentioned drift toward their standards and their ways of doing things.

### TOPICS FOR GROUP DISCUSSION

1. How account for the rapid numerical growth of the Baptist people?

2. Resolved, that Roger Williams has been a more potent influence for good in our national life than has the Puritanism with which he came into conflict.

3. Discover why the membership of Baptist churches is so largely composed of " the common people."

4. Is there a point beyond which pure democracy fails to yield desired results? If so, where is that point and how may its lack of fruitage be overcome?

5. Laying aside prejudice, raise the question as to whether eleven generations of history do actually vindicate the Baptists and their polity.

6. Question the author's explanation of why Baptist churches are not notably successful in our great centers of population. How will the group account for the fact?

7. What is the ultimate test of divine approval of a church, its polity, and program?

# *Polity and Practice in Baptist Churches*

## Books Worth Consulting

Newman, Albert Henry, *A History of the Baptist Churches in the United States.* The American Baptist Publication Society, Philadelphia, 1898.

Torbet, Robert G., *A History of the Baptists.* The Judson Press, Philadelphia, 1950; revised 1955.

Vedder, Henry C., *A Short History of the Baptists.* The American Baptist Publication Society, Philadelphia, 1907.

## Practical Suggestions

"Make history thy teacher," is counsel better than which was never given. Baptists, now the possessors of some three hundred and fifty years of active history, need to become students of those swift centuries. They need to familiarize themselves with the highway down which they have come in order to discover inspiration and marching orders for the tomorrows. They ought to seek to learn why some eleven generations have come to honor them as a people assured that for like reasons the future will yield a similar gratitude and esteem.

The Baptist fathers were men greatly in earnest about religion, as they conceived it. They suffered often for their tenets, because they believed them worth the suffering; a conviction vindicated by history, the final arbiter of truth. It becomes their children to nurture that religious zeal born of wisdom, and to be stedfast in loyalty to convictions likely to be crowned by the history that is to be.

These, the fathers in the faith, worked out their religious destiny under the banner of soul liberty. The recognition of this great principle they won from stubborn times, and passed it on to this generation as a priceless heritage. They bought it at the cost of suffering, even death. It behooves their sons and daughters to receive it as a treasure in golden vessels. But only to receive is not enough; these must carry forward, and in this day grow the richer fruits of that religious freedom which is born of soul competency. From this generation we ought to expect the outlawry of every sectarianism, religious bigotry, and attempt of anyone to coerce another; and the union of all in guaranteeing to each the full right to do his own thinking, to grow his own spiritual life and worship God as he chooses. In other words, present-day descendants of the pioneer Baptists—if true to the fathers—will strike for the only kind of religious unity ever possible, the unity in that spirit which respects every other man's quest for God, and rejoices in each good and ennobling finding that he makes. Thus may they be used of the Father of mankind to enrich Christianity and establish good-will in all the earth.

# V

## OFFICIALS IN BAPTIST CHURCHES

### Ministerial Education

The minister of the local church heads its official family. By grace of the church that calls him to its leadership he is *ex-officio* member of all boards, groups and committees within the organization.

The task of the modern minister is such as to demand a very fine type of specialist. He is challenged to be a specialist in the realm of growing souls. Far beyond the gardener who grows delicate and gorgeous flowers, he must not be a bungler. He must know his task even as engineers, physicians, and merchants know theirs. Herein lies the demand for a long and special preparation. Into his hands are to fall the divine resources, the unspeakable riches of the gospel of Christ, to dispense them so that the lives of youth, adult, and age may find their places in those processes that lead toward the abundant life as it was manifested in the Master himself. A high and holy responsibility belongs to the minister, and he who has the understanding heart will scarcely venture upon its duties without having—at least by exposure—availed himself of the vast resources of wisdom and culture accumulated by the ministry through more than sixty generations. The richest possible background and the fullest possible training are none too good to lay upon the altar of Him whom we serve. In other words, the work in hand earnestly asks a thorough education on the part of the worker, as quite the equal essential of full consecration.

# Officials in Baptist Churches

A major unit in such training is a four-year course in a high-grade college or university. Such years afford two items of unspeakable value to the prospective minister: mental discipline and an introduction to the accumulated wisdom of the race. What a difference between the disciplined and the undisciplined mind! The one goes straight and clean as an arrow to its mark, the other gyrates all about the premises. The writer once allowed a young woman—a graduate student in a near-by university—ten minutes preceding his Sunday morning sermon to present the cause of the Near East Relief. She finished in exactly nine and one-half minutes, and without one superfluous word or gesture had presented an admirable case for her cause. It was a fine exhibition of a trained mind in action. Another instance. Again a young woman was to present a cause dear to her heart and to the church in whose pulpit she was a guest. Forty minutes had been arranged for both her presentation and the sermon, she to consume not more than fifteen of the forty. She arose and began to ramble about, talking more or less interestingly, but revealing little or no organization of her material. The inevitable happened; she took thirty-six of the forty minutes, was greatly embarrassed, when, looking at her watch, she discovered what she had done, and sat down in humiliation. She had a good mind, but lacked training. And it is training that is required in the good minister; a finely trained and disciplined mind. Four years in a standard college may not guarantee such a mind, but they should help produce it.

Not only should the sickle be sharp; a good crop of grain is also most desirable. So, while a college course may discipline the mind of the minister, what is quite as essential is that it enrich his life with that knowledge and culture content upon which that well-instructed mind is to work. Such a goal looks to the college curriculum. It should guide the prospective minister into a basic knowledge of Latin, the language on which the English roots itself; a large acquaintance with the fields of history, literature, education, and the natural and social sciences; and a good foundation in psychologic and philosophic thought. Thus having begun let him turn to the theological seminary for that specialized training designed to fit him for his high calling.

Both in college and in the seminary the licentiate should be under the watch-care of his home church. The well-conducted theological seminary seeks not only the endorsement of the young man by his church, but its continuing interest in him. The wise choice of seminary on his part is even more important than the selection of a college; and in this choice his church should take a lively interest. By this stage in his education the student should have begun rigorous thinking on his own account; a seminary must be found that will encourage, inspire and guide that process. For in these three or four precious years he must acquaint himself with the field of religion in a way comparable to the specialist in law, engineering, economics, or medicine. His seminary must be one that will lead him to think his way into the mazes of contemporaneous religious thought, and then out again, so that he will be able to say with Paul, " *My* gospel." His own religion and his own message it has become because he has wrought it out in the deeps of his own life. Such a minister may stand before the world unabashed, because in his soul he can say, " This I know, because I have tested it." And such a minister may have large hope of winning the confidence and respect of the thoughtful persons of his parish.

Baptists have not always insisted on an educated ministry. There have been groups who opposed the education of their leaders, on the ground that when educated, "they lose the fire." Of course. The more a man is educated and the wider his fund of knowledge, the more modest he becomes. The educated man is generally a moderate man. He knows enough to take measure of his own lack of knowledge, and to walk humbly before God and men. "Fire," cock-sureness, omniscience, and uncurbed zeal are the general stock in trade of the ignorant.

However, the approval of such qualities is passing among Baptists. That attitude takes wings just as soon as general education comes among the rank and file of the people. And today few bodies of Christians—we choose to think—are better equipped than Baptists to guide the young man in the processes of a thorough theological training. They will expect the seminary to offer him the vision wide and high, to create in him the open, hungry mind, to set his feet in the long, patient road, and stedfastly commend to him the daily companionship of Him who walks there, with all who diligently seek the heights.

The wisest polity among Baptists recommends ordination only at the end of the candidate's formal training; that is to say, at the end of his seminary course. The assumption is that by this time some church will have extended him a call to become its pastor, and will ask for his ordination very soon after he is located on the field. This practice commends itself on the grounds that it not only retains the earlier custom of setting apart one as the minister of the ordaining church specifically, but also in that it constitutes a safeguard against the ordaining of those whom no church has called, is likely to call, or can call with any degree of safety.

The wisdom of this polity is commending itself increasingly to the churches, as is manifest by the fact that a multitude of associations and some State conventions have adopted fairly adequate standards of ordination, and the still further fact that the matter is a perennial item for consideration in the general conventions.

The reasons for this increased attention to standards are not far to seek. In the first place, we note the sure rise of the general educational level of the people in the pews; they grow impatient with, and even intolerant of, ignorance in the pulpit. Few churches can be found that do not enroll one or more college graduates, and these demand a minister with a training at least equal to their own. In the second place, various causes have contributed to an overcrowding in the ministry: the flooding of the professions; the rapid increase of the number of college graduates; the difficulties and uncertainties of the economic world; the tendency of churches to combine rather than to swarm, and the undue multiplying of so-called "Bible schools" and other short-cut institutions. This means competition and the consequent lowering of standards. Baptists, moreover, are peculiarly liable to get the culls and left-overs from other religious bodies, since their polity is weak in controls—they have no sure method of keeping out the undesirable. In the third place, the postwar period has been notable for a wave of devastating controversy, among whose results is the greatly increased number of the partisan and controversial. Such tend to be poorly trained, and are too uniformly divisive in their church relationships. All these conditions are conspiring to make stricter standards for ordination imperative.

The writer was present, not long since, at the annual meeting of the Pittsburgh Baptist Association when the two following standards of ordination were adopted. They are given here since they are typical of the standards being generally adopted. The first deals with those who come from other denominations seeking ordination; the second with the ordination of young men from Baptist churches.

I. The Permanent Council is often called upon to consider the fitness of men of other denominations who seek ordination at our hands. Heretofore there have been few, if any requirements imposed upon them except that they shall pass a satisfactory examination by the Council. It is manifestly impossible for the Council to ascertain all the information that ought to be in its possession before the vote on ordination has been taken, unless some preliminary investigation has been made. Therefore it seems desirable and reasonable to expect that such candidates should be required to make suitable preparation of themselves and furnish acceptable credentials before their names shall be presented to the Council by the Executive Committee.

In order to meet this situation, it is hereby suggested that the following requirements be imposed upon those who ask that we adopt them into our fellowship by way of ordination:

1. That the candidate be required to submit a statement in writing as to his reasons for seeking ordination into the ranks of the Baptist ministry.

2. That he submit a statement of his educational advantages.

3. That he be asked to give a record of his work in the denomination to which he now belongs. That it include a list of the churches he has served as pastor, his work as an evangelist and his work in general.

4. That he submit the names of at least three pastors, secretaries, or other leaders of his denomination who may be able to testify as to his character.

5. That every such candidate be required to read carefully the following documents on Baptist history and polity:

*The Baptist Manual,* Hiscox or Soares.
*Short History of the Baptists,* Vedder.
*The Second Survey,* or other statements of that character.
Constitution and By-Laws of the Pennsylvania Baptist General Convention.
Charter, Constitution and By-Laws of the Pittsburgh Baptist Association.

6. That each such applicant shall serve acceptably as the minister of a recognized Baptist church for at least one year preceding his public recognition as a Baptist minister.

II. We of the Council believe that the ordination of a candidate into the Baptist ministry concerns both the church which ordains and all the churches of the denomination, because a candidate ordained by a local church will presumably serve other churches, and enjoy the permanent benefits of membership in the Baptist ministry. For this reason we believe that any ordaining church will recognize its fraternal obligations to be advised by a regular, permanent or called council of the Association or State to which the church belongs or in whose territory the church is located, and by such ordination committee as the State Convention or Association may maintain. We believe that the church and council should keep in mind the following desirable considerations:

1. That the candidate be of unblemished character and irreproachable reputation, and that a moral obligation rests upon the Council to consider and if necessary investigate these matters.

2. That the candidate give evidence of genuine conversion and spiritual life.

3. That the candidate be of sound judgment and fitness of personality.

4. That the candidate give evidence of a clear and definite inward call from God to the Christian ministry, and that each candidate before ordination shall be a pastor or pastor-elect or under appointment for missionary or educational service, or give sufficient evidence of a genuine prospect of service in the ministry.

5. That the candidate should meet one of the following standards of preparation, here presented in order of preference:

[ 78 ]

(a) Standard college and standard theological studies, with graduation.

(b) Standard theological studies, with graduation, besides two years of college study.

(c) In the case of persons who for substantial reasons are unable to meet the above requirements, a substitute preparation, including full high school work, and at least two years of full study in a theological school or its well-recognized equivalent.

6. That strong approval should be given to the general custom of theological seminaries by which they refuse to participate, except under extraordinary circumstances, in the ordination of a student before his graduating year of theological study.

7. That every candidate for ordination to the Baptist ministry ought to be able to declare himself with biblical clearness and conviction upon the following subjects:

(a) God.

(b) The Person of Christ.

(c) The Gospel Message.

(d) The Church and Its Ordinances.

(e) The Candidate's knowledge and attitude regarding the Great Commission and Baptist world-wide missions.

### ORDINATION

Ordination is by the local church. It ordains one who is within its membership, and one who preferably is to be its own minister. The ceremony of ordination is a public "setting-apart" of the candidate to the ministry of Christ and his gospel. Details of the ordination program are in the hands of the ordaining church, in consultation with the candidate to be ordained and a committeeman from the examining council.

Theoretically the local church has complete authority in the matter of ordination, but in practice few churches assume to act independently. Ordinarily a given church is in fellowship with other Baptist churches, through the Association, or otherwise, and consequently it seeks their counsel in the important matter under consideration. This seeking of counsel is furthered by another important fact, namely, that a man once ordained becomes either an asset or liability *to all the churches.* Hence few churches are willing to take full responsibility for the contemplated ordination. Other and neighboring churches are requested to send representatives, including their ministers, to form an examining council which shall determine the fitness of the candidate for the high calling of a minister in Christ.

With growing frequency such a council is permanently organized and is representative of all the Baptist churches within the given Association. Such a permanent council has such officers and committees as it may itself determine, and usually meets annually at the time of the associational gathering for the election of officers and the transaction of other business. Special meetings are called whenever any church desires the counsel of the other churches relative to any matter, such as ordination.

Before this council the candidate is requested to appear for examination. The inquiry aims to ascertain the genuineness of his " Christian experience," the reasonableness of his " call to the ministry," and the acceptability of his " views of Christian doctrine." The relative importance given to these items depends of course upon the composite mind of the council. The ideal is that sufficient types of mind will be represented so as to secure a fair and genuine examination at all three points. Manifestly, an overstressing of any one of them at the expense of the others defeats the purpose for which the council has been convened. An objective evaluation of the three rates them in the order named: Christian character, first; a challenging call, second; conformity in doctrinal views, third. Baptists with their slogan of "soul liberty" logically have never been strong for conformity.

The examination concluded, a vote determines whether or not to advise the inquiring church to proceed with ordination.

Caution is the mood that becomes a church when it contemplates ordination. None would question its right to ordain a minister, *for itself*. Here the local church is regarded as wholly competent. But that it is competent to ordain *for others* is not granted. And just here arises urgent need for caution; for when the man is ordained he may then circulate throughout the denomination; and should he prove unfit for the ministry, he will be a continuing embarrassment to the church that ordained him and a burden to all the churches. This consideration makes it incumbent upon any church which has any semblance of fair-mindedness to seek the sanction of all the churches of its local Association before it proceeds to ordain.

Ordination is held by Baptists to do nothing magical or sacramental to the minister; it is only a formal way of setting him apart for a particular work among the churches. Ordination empowers him to administer the ordinances of baptism and the Lord's Supper, and in general to perform the services of a good minister. Beyond these matters ordination is held not to vest any power in him not resident in any other church-member. "Conduct unbecoming a minister" is considered sufficient ground for the church that holds his membership —upon the advice of a regularly constituted council of churches—to revoke his credentials.

# Polity and Practice in Baptist Churches

## SETTLING A PASTOR

As the local church is competent to ordain, so it is also competent to call and dismiss its own minister. A pastorless church in quest of a man to shepherd the flock has no definite polity to guide it. Every method conceivable is in operation in the denomination. The greatest confusion and utter lack of studied procedure reign at this crucial point. The rapid increase of ministerial supply makes it incumbent that the churches now work out some efficient and dignified method of finding the desired man and of extending the call. Lack of a stable polity creates a condition unfair to the ministry and hazardous for the churches. Having regard to this present confusion, we venture to offer the following procedure for adoption by the churches, a procedure which in part or in whole has been employed with considerable frequency.

Let us suppose that the minister has resigned and that on a certain date the pulpit will be vacated. As soon as his resignation is accepted, the church should appoint a pulpit committee, composed of men and women from its membership who have a reputation for wisdom and devotion. This committee should be charged with the responsibility of seeking out and presenting to the church in due season one whom they adjudge worthy to become the new leader. As soon as it is appointed let this committee meet in unhurried session, and after seeking divine guidance, proceed to organize by choosing a chairman and secretary. Then let it carefully plan a detailed method of procedure for itself, forthwith publishing the same to the church, so that all may understand and accord cooperation. The following will serve as a guide to such a pulpit committee:

# Officials in Baptist Churches

Your recently appointed pulpit committee has adopted the following points as guide to its procedure relative to the task assigned:

1. To invite immediately to the pulpit and pastoral function, as ad interim minister, someone not a possible candidate.

2. To present to the church as a candidate only such an one as is proved, after thorough investigation of his past record and his standing in the denomination, to be a man of Christian character above question or reproach, and who has been hitherto uniformly successful.

3. To present as a candidate only that man whom the committee has heard preach in his own pulpit and observed at work among his own people, and concerning whom the committee is a unit in believing to be the minister needed by the church at the present juncture.

4. To present to the church only one candidate at a time, urging that he be accepted or rejected. If the latter eventuates, to seek another in accordance with the foregoing procedure.

5. To make haste slowly, assured that all will be well under guidance of the ad interim minister, thus giving ample time to locate a minister suited to the present need.

We know of one State convention that has a committee making a careful study of polity now operative in settling a minister. We make the guess that their report will approximate the above. Should our churches uniformly proceed in accord with these suggestions they would do a genuine service to the ministry as well as themselves. Let us submit these paragraphs to scrutiny.

*The Ad Interim Minister.* Few churches are so located that they cannot immediately obtain the services of some minister not in the active pastorate who will cherish the opportunity to come to them for a season. More than likely he will be a retired minister, of experience and of good record for grace and wisdom. His immediate settlement will go far to keep the church on the even tenor of its ways, undisturbed by the change of pastorates. In addition, it will facilitate the work of the pulpit committee by leaving it free and unhurried in its quest, and relieving it of the necessity of arranging a "hearing" for some friend or relative of this, that, and the other member of the church. Moreover, it cools down the fever of competition on the part of many who are seeking placement.

*Thorough Investigation.* A pulpit committee who at all senses their responsibility will make a very thorough investigation of any minister whom they seriously consider recommending to the church. They will seek to know his religious, educational, and cultural backgrounds; they will inquire into his family life, and his standing in communities where he has served; they will look into his record in the churches to which he has ministered: Is he sincere, wise, nobly religious, non-divisive, a genuine leader whom success has crowned? They should ascertain his standing among his fellow ministers and with denominational leaders. In brief, the committee should leave no stone unturned to assure itself that they are considering a man in every sense worthy of his high calling and of their pastorate. To this procedure no minister will object whose record is what it should be. He will welcome the white light of such investigation.

*Committee Visitation.* When preliminary investigation and the general reputation of a minister lead the committee to think him worthy of possible consideration as a candidate, it should be its aim to visit his parish and church, unannounced, and, if possible, unobserved, in order to see him among his people and hear him in his own pulpit. If the initial visit gives encouragement, he should be heard on subsequent occasions, by different members of the committee, in the hope of confirming the favorable impression of the earlier visit. Not infrequently his present parish will be too far distant for the proposed visitation. In such case some one committee member may be designated to make the visit (at the church's expense, if necessary!). Or again, friends of committeemen living near may be asked to visit his field and report their findings. In yet other instances, some church not too far distant from the church seeking a pastor may be asked to invite the minister in question to be their guest preacher on a given Sunday. This will afford opportunity for the committee to hear him, perhaps in company with a few other members of the church whom they may care to invite.

If such hearings are favorable, and if the investigation from other angles is confirmatory, and the committee is agreed on this man, then the time has arrived to begin direct negotiations with the minister himself. Such negotiations should ascertain if he is favorable to a change of field; if he is in a position to consider a call, and if so, at what salary; and in case of a call, at what time he could assume pastoral relations. Supposing all this serves to confirm the committee in its initial unanimity, arrangements should be made for him to visit the vacant field as a candidate, preaching on Sunday, and when possible remaining for the mid-week service. Within ten days thereafter the church should vote upon the matter of extending a call. Should the vote be unfavorable, which is unlikely, the committee must begin its work anew, proceeding as before.

*One Candidate at a Time!* A wise committee will exert its full authority to nurture the unity of the church. Therefore it will not permit a multiplicity of candidates at one time. Its members will insist upon one candidate only, and that he be the one whom they recommend. In numberless instances other policy has proved the height of folly.

*Make Haste Slowly.* Cautious, unhurried action should be the watchword of the committee. To guarantee this it will have provided for an ad interim minister. The wisdom of this we have already indicated. We counsel caution because often the best of men is unsuited to certain fields, and because—sad as it is to relate—there are ministers whose records are such as to make it most hazardous for any church to extend them a call. We commend unhurried action because time is required to winnow from the numbers whose names will reach the committee the two or three whom it should care to consider; and still more time to follow out the several lines of investigation necessary in the case of these. There will be members of the church impatiently urging the committee to speedy action. It must refuse to be hurried, stedfastly staying by its policy to bring a candidate before the church only when it is a unit in so doing.

In this connection another word of caution needs to be given the pulpit committee, namely, that it beware of the temptation, having provided for an excellent ad interim ministry, to rest on its oars. Too long delay may discourage the church. And in any case, they need a regular minister, after reasonable delay. From six months to a year ought to terminate the temporary arrangement in favor of permanency.

A practice under guidance of the foregoing five principles would in time commend itself to our churches for its evident wisdom. Already such practice is employed by many churches that feel they can no longer take the hazards involved in a free-for-all campaign of candidating. Moreover, such procedure is compatible with the dignity and worth of the Christian ministry.

We must not forget that the pastorless period is critical for the church, while a churchless period may easily become tragic for the minister and his family. These evident and significant facts should be sufficient to compel Baptists to evolve a stable and becoming polity for bringing together the pastorless church and the worthy minister—the assumption being that said pastorless church is worthy of the worthy man of God.

Too long has "candidating" been the approved polity of the churches for "settling a minister." The day is overdue for a thoughtful scrutiny of the entire procedure. Let us enquire therefore if "candidating" is fair to the ministry.

Is it compatible with its spirit and dignity? Think of what it means: A minister is asked by an interested church to come and display himself, and his wares. Not only so, he is deliberately challenged by the invitation to "sell" himself to a congregation; not infrequently in competition with other ministers. He must demonstrate in an arena that his personal appearance, the quality of his voice, his platform ability and his social gifts are superior to all the others who have been or shall be before the church. Little wonder that many of our finest ministers have consistently refused to be put thus on the auction-block. It is a practice thoroughly humiliating to the more sensitive, and even the less sensitive.

Not infrequently circumstances seem to force a refined and cultured man into this humiliating display; he urgently desires to make a change of field, and is interested in the opportunity offered by a certain pastorless church. Then there comes an invitation to preach as a candidate. What shall he do? There is but one way open, namely, to accept the invitation, though he loathes the polity that makes it necessary. Under the strain involved the chances are that he will make a poor show-ing, and hence in the competition will lose to an inferior competitor. Few arrangements can be conceived more inimical to the advancement of the finest spirits among our ministers, for few such can rise above the candidating handicap. On the contrary, what an opportunity it does afford for the pulpiteer of the cheap-politician type! He would get nowhere by the method of merit and careful investigation, but he is a master at selling himself and the cheap line of goods he carries. Even when a church employs the more excellent judgment of having but one candidate before it at a time, hearing him and voting upon him before another is invited, even so the method is distasteful. We can scarcely think of the Master— were he a preacher on earth today—being a party to such a procedure. It is a phase of Baptist polity which grew up in the yesterdays, when means of communication and travel made it very difficult to look up a minister's record, or if he lived at any distance, to hear him preach. To invite him to come to the church for a day or a week was the most expeditious and the almost necessary way. But today there is no longer any necessity on such grounds. Happily, the churches are beginning to learn that the "candidating" method is universally disapproved by our better ministers—the kind they most desire as pastors.

But what of the church? Does the church prosper by such polity? Baptist history is eloquent in the reply: More churches have been injured by this practice than by any other single cause. Elmer Gantry always wins!

## Officials in Baptist Churches

We have known men who have made the journey from Maine to California—or the reverse—in the course of from ten to twenty years, leaving a trail of wrecked churches. By virtue of what? A polity that encourages a church to extend a call on the single consideration of apparent pulpit ability. In the light of the facts, all detrimental to the churches, such methods of securing a minister ought to be forthwith abandoned. All the more urgent becomes this admonition at a time when an oversupply in the ministry of practically all the denominations is likely to overflow the Baptists, who have no way of closing the flood-gates, even against the ignorant, the crassly crude, or the morally bad.

There should be launched forthwith a denomination-wide campaign designed to effect two things. First, to educate our churches as to how better to proceed when they must find new pastoral leadership; and secondly, to raise very decidedly the character and training standards for ordination, acquainting the churches with such standards. With the general education and culture of our people rapidly rising, we have more to fear from ignorant and untrained ministers than from any other source. No arrangement more apt to defeat the purposes of the Kingdom can be conceived than ignorance prating in the pulpit, the while education and good taste sit in the pew.

This polity of call and settlement, working today so very inadequately, places the ministers in a most delicate situation ethically. In earlier days there was an undersupply of ministers, hence for each, presumably, one or more churches were in waiting. At present it is not so. Then the minister desiring a change could show independence, and out of such evolve a high, non-competitive ethic; he could refuse to permit any church to place him in competition with a brother minister. The present oversupply of ministers has put him in competition, whether he will or not. Suppose one finds himself in urgent need to make a change of field; how may he ethically seek another pulpit? They are few, even among the more prominent, who can assume to say, " I shall permit no competition," if indeed he hopes for a call. Shall he write a business-like application for opportunity to investigate and consider a vacated field? Some of our wisest leaders say, yes; though with many pulpit committees that procedure would disqualify the man. What may he do, then; how may he proceed? Approved ministerial ethics is certain as to one proper procedure, namely, he should make known his wishes to ministerial and other friends who may care to intercede for him when a vacancy occurs. But this method will be entirely too slow for the " Reverend Elmer Gantry "; he will adopt the go-getter method—and very likely secure the call!

Churches that have ethical sense will have detected this delicate situation of the ministry, and will both espouse and practise a polity intolerant of competition and the consequent unethical practices fostered thereby. A church that, seeking a minister, will elect to adopt the procedure suggested earlier in this chapter can render a very distinct service to the ministry in that it thereby refuses to allow competition in its case or to be a party thereto. Forthright condemnation is the due of any church that fosters competition and its evil attendants. Recently our attention was drawn to a church that had actually applied the shady ethic of the business world to beat down the salary level of unemployed ministers. This surely constitutes sufficient ground for an Association to withdraw the hand of fellowship from such a church.

It remains to give a paragraph to Baptist polity as it functions in vacating a pulpit. As a church extends the call, so can it terminate the pastoral relationship. Fair dealing is entrusted—and very rarely with regret—to the working of the Christian spirit in this matter. Pastor and people enter into a contract, a compact that transcends civil law, to live and labor together. When for any reason either wishes to terminate the relationship the other party is notified to that effect, and by mutual agreement a date set for its consummation. Usually a period of three months is allowed to elapse after notification, though not infrequently this is shortened or lengthened by mutual consent. It is the part of the church, when dismissing a minister, to go the second mile in its will to be Christian. The minister on his part will plan always to conclude his work with a grace and dignity worthy of his high calling under Christ. Departing, he will close the door gently behind himself, in order to leave a united church.

### DEACONS

Baptist polity grants to each church the right to create its own organization. Although this policy might seem to invite wide divergencies, it has actually eventuated in a commendable uniformity. For example, Baptist churches elect deacons, who democratically organize themselves and nurture the spiritual life of the church. Sometimes they act as the minister's cabinet, although this function is assumed more often by a larger group, called the " church council " or " advisory board." This group, acting only in an *advisory* capacity, is then the minister's cabinet, assisting him by counsel and close cooperation in all that is aimed to enlarge and enrich his ministry.

The foregoing indicates the significance of this official and at the same time points out necessary qualifications. These are not, in ideal, other than those for the good minister. First of all, he should be a good man in all his ways, an exemplar of Christ in every phase of his life. He should be a man with education equal to or above the average of the church-membership; and be known among the people as wise and of gracious moderation. The board of deacons is to the church what a sound heart is to the physical man.

Deacons are democratically elected by the church at a regularly constituted meeting, usually the church's annual meeting. Wise practice decrees that nominees for this important office be placed before the meeting by a nominating committee appointed some weeks previously. Churches that proceed with caution and wisdom thus prohibit the unstudied and miscellaneous nominations that are certain to come from the floor. It is best that the committee nominate only the number to be elected, since to do otherwise is to make necessary the defeat of the excess number; and this has too evident dangers to be at all permitted.

Tenure of office for deacons has and does vary widely. In this matter the local church is its own authority. Formerly the custom of ordaining deacons—much as a minister is ordained—was wide-spread. Such a practice seemed to comport with the importance and dignity of this official, from which point of view it is worthy of commendation. Other churches, for the same reasons, elect for life; and such a member when being dismissed by letter to another Baptist church is dismissed as a deacon. The hope thus expressed is that the receiving church may find it desirable to take him into its diaconate. On this point of life-tenure, however, our polity has been making a very marked shift. Though exercising the greatest care, many churches have found themselves embarrassed by having extended life-tenure to a man unfitted for or unworthy of the high office. And so here the strength that has always obtained in Baptist polity—the ready ability to change in face of need—has revealed itself by instituting limited tenure. In our judgment, the wisest contemporary practice establishes rotation in office in the board of deacons, one third or one-fourth of its members being elected every year (we prefer the three-year tenure), with no retiring member being able to succeed himself until the expiration of at least one year. This happily unites stability with change in such ratio as to secure efficiency and harmony.

Let us interject here an endorsement of the policy of rotation throughout the whole organizational life of the church. General rotation is on the increase among the churches and is uniformly commending itself. It puts every officer on tiptoe to busy himself at his task, seeing that he has but a limited period in which to complete it. Moreover, it gives others opportunity to exercise their gifts and to grow thereby. Most churches addicted to the life-tenure polity have at some time or other had occasion to regret it. To avoid offense they have been compelled to sit by and see some phase of their work suffer. If there are cases where limited tenure might seem detrimental—church school superintendents, for example—let the tenure of office be lengthened to, say, five years. Such a period will permit the capable officer to do a good, constructive work, and will be long enough to endure the incompetent. When rotation in office is the policy of a church, adopted by vote of the membership, it avoids all the vexing possibilities of long-term or life-tenure.

An increasing number of churches parallel the board of deacons with a board of deaconesses, composed of good and capable women—not infrequently wives of the deacons—who assist the latter in their work. We feel assured this practice will justify itself and grow ultimately into a feature so stable as to be an accepted part of Baptist polity. Should the question of New Testament authority be raised, it is sufficient to submit that one of the two guiding principles of New Testament polity is its fluidity or adaptability to meet new needs. Churches, therefore, that see a need which they think can be best met by deaconesses are entirely scriptural in appointing them.

## TRUSTEES

A second major board of Baptist churches is that of trustees. It is composed of lay people, elected by the church as are the deacons. They are charged with the responsibility of promoting the physical welfare of the church. Their two major tasks are to care for the church property, invested funds, and the like, and to finance the work of the church. The nature of the tasks assigned to this board indicates the type of men and women required. They should have a genuine interest in and sympathy for the work, and broad experience in business and financial affairs. Here, as elsewhere, rotation in office is desirable since it guarantees the open door of a training school to other members and prevents the board from becoming a closed corporation. Those responsible for the finances should be among the most interested and alert, else the whole enterprise may be handicapped. Both the treasurer of current expense funds and the treasurer of benevolence moneys should be elected by the church, but made ex-officio members of the board of trustees.

The second named phase of the task of the trustees is not wholly established. Many trustees consider it their whole duty to receive and hold church property and money; they have not faced up to the more difficult task of producing the funds necessary to the church's program. They ought to educate the members as to financial needs, show how and why the money is expended, set up and promote the every-member canvass, or whatever method seems to them designed to secure the best results, both in creating the benevolent spirit and in securing money adequate to provide for the needs; and in general to see to it that the program and work suffer at no point for lack of funds.

## Board of Education

The chief educational officer, aside from the minister, has been the church school superintendent. Generally he has not been considered an officer of the church so much as of the school itself. Soundest polity, however, makes him an actual church officer, elected by the church, and by it charged with the task of directing the work of its school. This statement should be qualified in the case of the comparatively few churches where he works under the supervision of an employed director of religious education.

Many churches maintain—very wisely we think—a third major board, namely the board of education. The function of this body is broadly indicated by its name. Its members, elected by the church, are carefully chosen and because of special qualifications. Such a board be-

comes the superior council of education and in cooperation with officers and teachers creates policy and program,
and generally nurtures the educational ideal throughout
the church. This practice is on the increase and bids
fair to crystallize into polity during the next generation.
Its promise is great and encouraging.

Any photograph of Baptist polity is sure to be a composite, since polity is ever in the making. Only *in general*
is there uniformity. Regarding officers, the direction
of growth today is more and more to make them *definitely
officers of the church.* The church is one, though it hus-
bands many interests and activities. Hence not only
deacons and trustees, but also church school executive
officers, and also those of the young people's society, the
men's union, the women's association, are all elected by
the church at the annual meeting, and are, accordingly,
responsible to the church. Often, indeed, they are actually nominated by the group most interested, yet they
come before the church as nominees of its nominating
committee. In their case, too, the principle of rotation
in office is commending itself.

### BOARD OF MISSIONS

Paralleling other boards is the Board of Missions, a
body of more recent origin. It is being incorporated into
the organizational structure of an increasing number of
churches. Like other groups, its members are elected by
the church, giving it the importance of a Church Board.
As its name implies, its function is to nurture and promote
missionary interests throughout the church.

### EDUCATION OF OFFICERS

Already this chapter has grown beyond allotted bounds,

yet we would note a corollary of the above considerations, namely, the need of special training for church officials. Polity with regard to this cannot be said to exist; only in rare cases are the churches sensing the need, and beginning to plant the seed for this new item of polity. For instance, here is a church whose minister is proposing definitely to offer some training for each group of officers. His program for the deacons consists of three hours of lecture and discussion, on the theme, "The Place and Function of the Board of Deacons." In addition, he has selected books which he distributes, asking individuals to review them at the regular monthly meetings of the board. And this same informative program he promotes for officers throughout the church. This type of education, for those in office and those likely to be, is fundamentally sound and to be commended. For surely nothing is more detrimental than to have important portions of a church program fall into the hands of those who are largely ignorant of what is expected of them. The evident remedy is education—and education *in advance* of accepting the responsibility of office.

### Topics for Group Discussion

1. Believing the gospel of our Lord Jesus Christ to be the most precious thing in the world, should any save the educated be encouraged to advocate it and apply it to the minds and hearts of men?

2. What standards do American Baptists erect as prerequisite to ordination? How may the churches be persuaded to insist on meeting these ideals before they proceed to ordain? Do Southern Baptists differ in practice?

3. How should a pastorless church proceed to secure an-

other minister? A churchless minister desires a field of labor; what may he do about it?

4. Name the chief boards or standing committees found in most Baptist churches. Describe their organization. Indicate the proper function of each.

5. Evaluate the suggestion of rotation in office. How could it be made operative in your own church, providing it were desirable?

BOOKS WORTH CONSULTING

Asquith, Glenn and the Department of Evangelism of the American Baptist Home Mission Societies, *The Work of Deacons, Deaconesses, and Evangelism Committee*. The Commission on Lay Development, American Baptist Convention, Philadelphia, 1958.

Asquith, Glenn, *Church Officers at Work*. The Judson Press, Philadelphia, 1951; revised 1952.

Crossland, Weldon, *Better Leaders for Your Church*. The Abingdon Press, Nashville, 1955.

Dolloff, Eugene Dinsmore, *The Efficient Church Officer: His Responsibilities and Problems*. Fleming H. Revell Co., New York, 1949.

Kirk, Kenneth E., *The Apostolic Ministry*. Morehouse-Gorham Co., New York, 1946.

Latourette, Kenneth Scott, *The Christian World Mission in Our Day*. Harper and Brothers, New York, 1954.

Smart, James D., *The Teaching Ministry of the Church*. The Westminster Press, Philadelphia, 1954.

Stevens, Dorothy, *Missionary Education in a Baptist Church*. The Judson Press, Philadelphia, 1953.

Torbet, Robert G., *The Baptist Ministry: Then and Now*. The Judson Press, Philadelphia, 1953.

# Officials in Baptist Churches

Whitehouse, Elizabeth, *Opening the Bible to Children.*
The Bethany Press, St. Louis; revised, 1955.

### PRACTICAL SUGGESTIONS

Dignify the entire work of religious education in your
church by creating, in the Constitution of the church, a
Board of Education. Let it be composed of the best qualified men and women in the membership; and insist that
it be set up by vote of the church. Moreover, its duties
and responsibilities should be specified by the church. In
the main these should consist in coordination of all educational projects; the maintaining of high standards; seeing that capable officers are selected, that a staff of teachers is in training to become better teachers, and in general,
to make the whole Christian educational process in the
church equal to that in the public schools.

Few need be convinced that the most significant advance within the churches of our day is in the field of
religious education. The schools of the church have
better equipment, better direction and better quality of
teaching than ever before. Genuine progress is being
made all along this front, and the more forward-looking
leaders are coming to view the total work of the church as
a soundly educational project. This viewpoint intimates
the great importance of a genuinely capable board such
as we suggest.

If Christian education be defined as *the direction of
growth toward Jesus Christ and his kind of life,* then it
becomes clear that no work of the church may be less
than educational, perhaps none can be more. Whether in
school or pulpit, whether at home or abroad, the educational ideal holds every builder of the Kingdom up to his
finest and best effort.

## VI

## THE MATTER OF AUTHORITY

An honored teacher prayed, " Father of men, spare us the necessity of always being logical." That petition is affirmatively answered in most of us. We habitually hold little intercourse with logic. Note our reactions in the case of authority and freedom; in certain mood we cry to heaven for freedom, and in other mood seek the safe harbor of authority. Men volunteer to die to secure certain liberty; having won it they flee from its responsibilities, turning back toward their former estate. It is as though all men had fallen under the spell of two opposite poles, and migrating back and forth between the two they spend their days as a shuttle. They are drawn now to the pole of freedom, and then hurled back toward that of authority. Take the case of Baptists who have quite uniformly pitched their tents toward the liberty-of-conscience pole, but at times have retreated in haste to some sheltering authority. On their banners have always been emblazoned such shibboleths as " soul competency," " religious liberty," " soul freedom," " voluntariness," " freedom of conscience," and " the priesthood of believers," but these banners have often been dipped—when some authority passed by.

In other phrase, the matter of authority has constituted a perennial problem for the Baptists. Their regulative idea of the competency of the human soul in religion, when followed to the end of its logic, rules authority out of the pattern of life completely. While on the

19611

other hand the recognition of any absolute authority takes competency speedily to the cross and sepulcher. Here are manifest the two poles; and they stand as far apart as opposing eternities. No man can at one and the same time live under the dominance of both. Either the soul of man is competent or it is not. If it is competent, then coercive authority is anathema; if it is not competent then authority must be embraced. Which? Baptists stedfastly hold to competency, in theory; in practice, as far as possible. Most men find congenial atmosphere in the vicinity of some equator that runs midway between the poles.

When we come to grips with this problem it seems immediately necessary to ascertain what we are to mean by authority. Even casual thought concerning the problem reveals the fact that the word authority varies widely in meaning, that the concept is of the kind which may have one of many contents. For example, one may read that Euclid is an authority in geometry, or that Schweitzer is an authority on the pipe-organ. The reader understands that the authority in the mind of the writer is that of a wider and deeper knowledge than that possessed by most men, even most mathematicians and musicians. Or it may be said that St. Paul and St. Francis of Assisi each speaks with authority relative to the Christian manner of living, and the abundant satisfactions that come to the fully surrendered life. What is meant is that these godly men speak out of an experience with their Lord far more vital than that known to most of us who profess discipleship. Hence they speak with authority to us. Or it may be alleged that Athanasius is authority on the doctrines which are elemental in the historic creed that bears his name; or that Sir Christopher Wren is authority in that

H [ 101 ]

which pertains to the noble and dignified in church archi-
tecture. The meaning is clear; namely, that those who
have created or built something may therefore speak with
the authority of an enlarged experience. So, also, men
speak of the authority of the Bible, the authority of the
Westminster Confession, the authority of Jesus of Nazareth, or the authority of the eternal God and Father. It
is manifest that, as employed in these many cases, the
concept of authority runs a wide range of variance, all
the way from Euclid to God.

It turns out therefore, in the processes of growing a
life, that that is authority for one which he recognizes
as having the inherent right, in some degree, to command or control; the right to limit or direct in thought
and conduct. Such authority may extend all the way
from mild guidance to absolute control. For example,
on the authority of a much-traveled friend, one may
decide to spend a vacation on Martha's Vineyard. Or
again, a man may completely yield all his capacity and
power in obedience when he hears God speak. Between
these two authorities lie unnumbered authorities, differing
one from another in the degree of admitted right to order
the life. In this connection we observe that the Declaration of Independence makes a sage observation when it
heralds the doctrine, "All government derives its power
from the consent of the governed." The keyword there
is " consent." Is it not likewise true that all authority
derives its right to guide or control from the *consent* of
him who is to be guided or controlled? This is positively
the case if man is a competent soul; since if he cannot
choose his authorities his competency is only shadow and
not reality.

This truth, enunciated by the Declaration, is significant

regardless of the angle of one's approach to it. Among other things it provides the nexus between freedom and authority, competency and control. It lays a dissolving finger upon our so-called problem of authority. It indicates that man, competent to govern himself, may yet *yield* to the authority of constituted government the right which is inherently his. The principle thereby educed is quite as valid in the realms of morals and religion. The soul, fully competent to order its religious behavior, may also *choose* to yield to the ordering of another, which ordering to a permitted degree becomes an authority. Any authority, of whatever nature or degree, exercised without the consent and election of the governed is usurpation, and has degenerated into coercion. Even the government which proclaims that all governments derive " their just powers from the consent of the governed," finds itself acting in apparent contravention of its laudable tenet when it must coerce the recalcitrant individual or minority. It does so by proceeding upon the theory that government is the instrument of the majority and may therefore, with due restraint, exercise coercion when the welfare of the many is at stake.

From earliest days Baptists have sensed this principle, conceiving, however, that authority in religious matters may justly be exercised over a competent soul by and with his *consent* only. They have consistently denied the right of anyone to abrogate the principle, even in case of the non-conformist individual or minority (of course, since Baptists were usually in the minority!). Hence their doctrine of absolute religious liberty. This is the nub of the issue between New England Puritans and the recalcitrant Roger Williams, founder of the Providence Plantation; wherein absolute religious liberty was a basic guarantee—liberty, forsooth, to the point of license! Coercion in any form is anathema to the Baptist conscience. Not even God may coerce one of his children. And of course he never does. Jesus came, high Ambassador of God the Father, to exercise wide authority over men, but always and only when persuasion and sweet reasonableness had born the fruit of consent. God ever deals with men as patient Teacher, never as absolute Monarch. Having created men free, like himself and after his own image, they may depend upon it that he will never violate that freedom by any semblance of coercion. From this exalted position God cannot be moved, least of all by brazen atheist or ribald blasphemer.

Therefore let men feel secure in their freedom of soul before God. Let them be assured also of a soul competency adequate to the exercise of that freedom. And moreover, let them know that by and through that exercise alone they grow toward the fulness of the stature of the sons of God. If this be true—and we challenge denial—then there arises a nice question in the realm of authority, namely, When and to whom may one yield consent as to authority? In other words, since the Creator has crowned every man king over his own life, to whom may he abdicate? May one abdicate to another without chancing self-injury? Can it be thought that God even would accept one's throne, should that one voluntarily step aside, and there hold absolute sway? We cannot think so; man would thereby shirk that responsibility which is the *sine qua non* of his own growth, and the Father would at the same time defeat his own purpose in his developing child. It were better to feel him ever near one's throne; whether it be established in strength or tottering in weakness; there giving inspiration, wisdom and guidance to the end that the human empire may be brought into harmony with and incorporated into the kingdom of God.

So Baptists hold, and in the light of such reasoning they exercise their competency in the evaluation of any and all authorities which are proposed. Each sits calmly upon the throne of his own life and inquires, " To what extent do I wish to heed this one who now approaches with claims of authority? " And as he wishes he decides the fate of each suppliant. Though he be pope or bishop or other high ecclesiastic, he must convince of his authority and thus win consent to exercise it. He may perchance be granted some degree of authority in the realm of religion, as Luther Burbank was in that of cross-breeding and development of plants, or as Professor Rautenstrauch is concerning matters of technocracy. In no case will he be granted authority even approximating the absolute and final.

Proceeding thus, Baptists from earliest days have refused consent to civil authority to reach over into the religion world. In this world the magistrate is considered an intruder.[1] As good citizens they gladly yield to his rule in all affairs of state, the sphere of his proper authority. History makes plain that many of " this sect " paid with their lives for their devotion to this principle. Denial of the right of the magistrate to rule his conscience brought the banishment of Roger Williams from the Massachusetts Bay Colony. This historic issue, as we have noted elsewhere, has been galvanized into life again

[1] Article 14 of the New Hampshire Confession teaches " that magistrates are to be prayed for, conscientiously honored and obeyed, except only in things opposed to the will of our Lord Jesus Christ, who is the only Lord of the conscience and the Prince of the kings of the earth." And this because " civil rulers have no rights of control over, or of interference with, religious matters."

in our own day in the heralded Macintosh Case. Prof. Douglas Clyde Macintosh, of Yale University, being a Canadian citizen, applied for citizenship in the United States. The formalities proceeded apace until he was asked to make oath of his willingness to bear arms in defense of the country of his adoption. He refused to take such an oath. He did so on the ground that he was thereby required to mortgage his conscience in advance of the arising occasion for bearing arms. He was being asked to yield to authority without the right to consider the matter; in other words, he was being forced to abdicate in favor of one upon whom he might not pass judgment. Citizenship was refused; whereupon the case was appealed, and finally passed upon by the Supreme Court of the United States. The decision sustained the refusal of citizenship by a five-to-four vote. The minority opinion was handed down by Mr. Chief Justice Charles Evans Hughes, and was a learned vindication of the position taken by Professor Macintosh when he placed conscience above the requirement of civil authority. It is an interesting fact that both the Professor and the Chief Justice are Baptists, and were but voicing the historic position of their denomination. True to the principle under consideration, Doctor Macintosh willingly granted the right of the state to exercise authority over him in all civil matters, but bearing arms he conceived to lie essentially within the realm of morals and religion, wherein he could not and would not give consent to any external authority. The reverberations of this notable decision of the Supreme Court have been heard around the world wherever men cherish freedom, and it is not too much to expect that within twenty-five years, at the most, a reversal of the judgment will be made.

# The Matter of Authority

In the light of the foregoing one who runs may read the reasons why Baptists have neither created a creed nor made any one of the historic creeds their own.[2] Far from doing either, they are anticreedal in basic position. Neither their doctrine nor their polity has been able to stand the strain of a creedal hand. This is not because Baptists do not believe—and believe most of that embedded in the historic creeds—but because creeds have ever shown a peculiar tendency to gather to themselves authority, than which Baptists fear nothing more. American Baptists have demonstrated in recent years a stubborn unwillingness to adopt a creed even of their own making. To " adopt " seemed to carry authoritarian implications which are obnoxious to the free and those who have concern for the freedom of others. When a man is of the conviction that he alone is competent within his own religious life, he may be positively willing to die for his creed, and equally willing to die rather than accept the creed of another. As we have said before, competency places him upon the throne of his own life, and that throne he may not abdicate against his will. To be sure, he ought ever to be teachable; but never coercible; and creeds have a way of seizing coercive power. Though anticreedal in polity, the Baptist churches have quite uniformly adopted each its own confession of faith. These are original, or copied, as the church elects, and are for the most part statements of the doctrinal position of the local church.[3] In content they are in fact quite

---

[2] At the organization of the Southern Baptist Convention, in 1845, it was announced, " We have constructed for our basis no creed, acting in this matter upon a Baptist aversion for all creeds but the Bible."

[3] The so-called Philadelphia Confession is a copy of the Assembly Confession, or Second London Confession, promulgated in 1689 by English and Welsh Baptists; to this Philadelphia Baptists added two articles, borrowed from Keach's Confession.

creedal, but the name, " confession of faith," is intended
to imply very definitely that it is not a creed in the historic sense. Even so, safeguarded as they are against
creedal implications, these have sometimes been used to
coerce members or churches whose beliefs were thought
to be too widely variant from the majority. When confessions are elevated to a position of such authority, it is in
violation of the fundamental doctrine of competency; hence
polity decrees that a confession of faith must never abrogate to itself creedal prerogatives.

Baptists enroll themselves among those who would be
known as " Bible Christians." They have been and are
still pre-eminently a people of " The Book." From it they
seek guidance and to it they turn for instruction in terms
of divine wisdom. They have not infrequently become
excessive literalists, when the migratory movement has
set out in the direction of the authority pole; and quite
the opposite when the tide has turned, under the banner
of soul liberty, toward the other pole. This people,
harassed as all bodies of Christians are at times by the
problem of authority, has invariably found the Bible its
city of refuge. Hard pressed, they have reiterated a
historic phrase,* " The Bible is a sufficient authority and
guide in matters of faith and practice "—in matters of
doctrine, polity and conduct. How very often have the
friendly walls of that citadel given shelter and comfort
to both individual and group! From " The Book " how
often has light broken upon a troubled pathway, as competent souls have devoutly scanned its pages! For such

---

* " Resolved, That we reaffirm our faith in the New Testament as a divinely
inspired record and therefore a trustworthy, authoritative and all-sufficient
rule of our faith and practice. We rededicate ourselves to Jesus Christ as
Lord and Savior and call our entire denomination to the common task of
sharing the whole Gospel with the whole world." This resolution was passed
by the Northern Baptist Convention in 1946 and reaffirmed by it in 1949.

men and women there is thus gained a large liberty; liberty under control of what God says to each one as he reads and listens. Thus it is that they discover an authority which is a sufficient guide in all the major concerns of life.

In this deliverance is a very revealing clause, namely, " a sufficient guide."[4] The implication is unmistakable; the guidance is not foolproof, nor absolute. It is not such guidance as abrogates competency, or relieves the believer of the necessity of exercising his own capacities to the full. It is a guidance for him who fearlessly thinks, devoutly prays, and persistently plods on; but not sufficient for the religiously indolent or dull. It is that high and holy variety of guidance which comports with competency and calls out the best and keenest in men. The Bible is a divine charter of soul liberty, but a charter that lays upon those freed a heavy obligation, the obligation to seek earnestly and devoutly the will of God, and finding it to follow its dictates. In that will, and that alone, is reposed an authority to which the sovereign soul of the freed-man may freely and fully bow. But not every freed-man finds that will!

After all, it is not paper and ink that constitute a " sufficient guide "; it lies rather in those princely personalities who stride across the pages of the Book. From them the good and wise may find guidance. Each presents himself with a just claim of authority. Saul speaks with authority of the folly of the foolish, and David so speaks the wisdom of the wise; the prophets of Baal authoritatively proclaim the tricks of the false, while

---

[4] Typically, the Baptist Union of Great Britain and Ireland, in 1888, declares its belief in, " The Divine Inspiration and Authority of the Holy Scriptures as the supreme and sufficient rule of our faith and practice; and the right and duty of individual judgment in the interpretation of it."

Isaiah heralds the insights of a seer of the Eternal; Paul is the advocate of a challenging missionary zeal, while James warns of the death that lurks in a temporizing policy; but of all who emerge from the pages of Scripture One stands head and shoulders above them all, Jesus of Nazareth. In ethical insight and religious penetration he surpasses them all by centuries, if not by eternities. He speaks, in these realms, with what seems to us the voice of finality. When he has spoken we can discover no beyond. It is as though God himself had made a deliverance. When he presents credentials of authority to the competent soul, Baptists maintain that these may be, yes, ought to be, accepted at face value; and that such a soul is justified in yielding unabridged consent to this Lordship.

Even so, guidance in Christ remains only a "sufficient" guidance. Christ has not spoken on all ethical and religious issues that arise today, or that are indigenous to our modern world. The seeker after guidance ought so intimately to know the mind of Christ that he can confidently predict what Christ would say and do were he living today in the flesh and confronting our problems with us. After all, the seeker is thrown back upon the exercise of his competency measurably to understand the greatest Personality of the ages and to catch something of the breath of his spirit. Sufficient guidance? Yes, to be sure. Absolute guidance? By no means.

The Baptist position, it follows, leaves wide open a door for the teacher; but never for the authoritarian. There is ever place for and crying need for those who *have been with Jesus,* and with the religious seers of the ages; need for those who have spent time on the heights and have learned something about God, and who there-

fore can bring inspiration, courage and assurance to less
fortunate or younger seekers. Verily, there is great place
for the real teacher; one who offers instruction, who
modestly persuades, who sits as advocate before the bar
of the reason, who calls the will into noble action, who
breaks to the teachable the bread of life. For such teachers God calls, on behalf of his people. Those who intimi-
date and coerce he cannot use, of course; free souls may
not be so violated.[5]

Beyond question it is true that the age-long method of
God's dealings with men is precisely that which operates
between teacher and taught. For God has ever been the
Teacher. Whenever he sent king, priest, or prophet, it
was that they, on his behalf, might teach the people. These
were never commissioned to coerce; they were each and
all sent to win and so to lead. We believe that of all the
names by which Jesus was known, " Teacher " was closest
to his heart. He spoke with authority, undeniably, but it
was the authority of the teacher. He was a positive
teacher, but never dogmatic; invariably having stated
his own position, he turned—as becomes the genuine
teacher—to inquire, " What think ye?" What refined
caution he employed, never to violate the integrity of a
competent, free personality!

Baptist polity has been projected from the outset to
make large room for the teacher and his ministry. Few
groups have been more forward than Baptists in matters
of education. In every land where their influence has
gone they have planted schools. They have commissioned
at once, and as companions, the teacher and the evangelist

[5] In the " Confession of Faith put forth by Elders and Brethren of many
Congregations of Christians in London and County," printed 1677, we read,
" God alone is Lord of the Conscience, and left it free from the Doctrines
and Commandments of men."

—both had been previously taught. Little faith has been shown in uninstructed zeal. Almost every State in the union has its Baptist college, founded originally for the training of ministers. Their outstanding ministers have always been teachers; men seeking to edify the people by sound teaching. The mere exhorter has never won an accepted and accredited place among the Baptist churches, though he has occasionally announced his coming and put in his appearance. In other words, Baptists have committed their whole progress to the hands of their teachers. In home, church, and mission field the policy is ever to teach and be taught. No authority beyond that of the good religious teacher is ever rightly desired. Hence they have gone " into all the world *teaching* them " to carry forward to consummation " the things which Jesus began to do and to *teach*."

Authority, as such, has a perfect genius for building systems of inhibition and control. Bestow upon a given center a measure of authority, even though it be a meager measure, and it will very soon begin to grow outreaching tentacles by means of which it draws to itself yet greater authority. Unless force or the grace of God intervene, the wondering eyes of men will behold the growth of an octopus of power before which fawning is appropriate.

They are many who place their hope for Christian unity in this outreaching and consolidating power of centralized authority. Baptists have never shared that hope. They have looked to the creation of a higher unity, born not of coercion but of freedom. They have put their trust in the spread of a conviction that the common man is not subject to the priest, but is his own priest. This " priesthood of all believers " Baptists hold to be a doctrine that bears within itself the possibilities of a cohesion transcending that to be secured by any coercive authority from the outside. Thus they make the sublime venture of faith in men, namely, that if men are left free and unhindered they will migrate, as by some centripetal force, toward a common center and a natural unity.

History, contrary to the prophecy of the authoritarian, vindicates this venture of faith. The doctrine of personal priesthood, instead of creating numberless individualists incapable of any cohesion or cooperation, has done quite the opposite. It has created a bond natural to free men, than which none stronger is known. It is doubtful if any large body of Christians today can display a more vital and living unity than that which holds together some twenty millions of Baptists. To be sure, there arise differences of opinion within the body, but this is indigenous to a democracy. If these did not arise it would be time to sound alarm, since it would indicate death. Freedom to express one's views in the assembly, or to participate in debate, is basic in Baptist polity. It is required only that the spirit of Christ continue to reign throughout the discussion. It is interesting to note that occasional periods of stress and disunity are uniformly precipitated and sustained by alleged attempts to coerce and control; attempts wholly foreign and antipathetic to Baptist genius.

Unity by way of democracy lies in the realm of idealism; and pure idealism is rarely attained in this world. But this may be said to its glory, namely, that such a unity must be achieved by dint of patient toil. It cannot be superimposed; it must be grown. Baptist unity is a case in point. As free and independent churches multiplied they had to learn the ways of cooperation. First came the association, wherein the churches felt their way forward with hesitancy. It was an untried path, and they moved with caution. Yet as they progressed the way came to seem not only good but much to be desired. And so, in the passing of the years they have moved forward, achieving the necessary unity as they advanced, coming finally into denominational and even world-wide oneness. Not only so, the way of cooperation has been found so compatible with local church freedom and so effective in the work of the kingdom of God that Baptists are today joining hands with churches of other name in thousands of communities; are cooperating with other denominations through the National Council of the Churches of Christ in the United States of America, and the World Council of Churches, thus participating in many world conferences. It has been discovered that there may be no limits to cooperative effort so long as freedom is maintained. Cooperation ends wherever and whenever coercion begins—at least it ends for Baptists.

## Topics for Group Discussion

1. First determine what is implied by authority; then discover the different kinds and degrees thereof.

2. Why is authority a problem more vexing for Baptists than for Roman Catholics, for example?

3. Why the separation-of-church-and-state doctrine? Set forth the case for and against its operation; for instance, in the field of religious education.

4. How harmonize the doctrines of the lordship of Jesus and that of the freedom of the soul?

5. Why the historic aversion of Baptists for creeds? Where have they found adequate standards for faith and practice?

6. Would it be wisdom to provide growing lives absolute and detailed rules for right conduct in every possible situation?

― 7. Is human progress desirable? Can there be progress under an authoritarian régime?

## Books Worth Consulting

Hastings, James, ed., *Encyclopedia of Religion and Ethics, 13 vols.* Charles Scribner's Sons, New York, 1951.

Jenkins, Daniel T., *Congregationalism: A Restatement.* Harper and Brothers, New York, 1954.

Johnson, Ralph M. and Goodwin, R. Dean, *Faith and Fellowship of American Baptists.* Council on Missionary Cooperation of the American Baptist Convention, New York, 1957.

Lumpkin, William L., *Baptist Confessions of Faith.* The Judson Press, Philadelphia, 1959.

## Practical Suggestions

Let each member of the group write a drama showing two ways of bringing up a boy. Two families of the same social class each have a two-year-old boy. One of these families is rigidly authoritarian and hence " lays down the law " for its growing boy on every occasion; the other family is sanely free, aiming to guide Junior's growing life by comradeship and the inculcation of challenging ideals. Have these boys meet as young men at college, competitors in classroom and in college activities, and therein show the points of character in each that win. Make this a study in contrasts. Let them meet again as citizens and homebuilders in a given community, and note the kind of citizen each is, the sort of home each builds, and the kind of church leader each becomes.

# VII

## THE ORDINANCES OF THE CHURCHES

By an ordinance is meant here a practice instituted by Christ and to be held in perpetuity by the churches that bear his name. Baptists believe that they are two in number, baptism and the Lord's Supper.

Jesus was himself baptized by John in the river Jordan and later urged the rite for his disciples. Apparently they followed his request on their own behalf, and administered it to new converts. It is recorded that a multitude were baptized at Pentecost. It is an interesting observation that Jesus himself never baptized anyone; it is explicitly stated that he did not. Nevertheless, his church has maintained the practice across these twenty centuries, with almost unvarying uniformity. The Friends are about the only exception among the Christian sects, they having eschewed all outward forms and ceremonies.

The second ordinance was instituted by our Lord in the upper room on the evening before his death. Here he and his disciples had assembled for the Passover meal, which turned out to be a meal of fellowship exceedingly rich and tender; their last meal together. At its close, and as a climax to these never-to-be-forgotten hours, he instituted what we have come to call the Lord's Supper. Others of the faith refer to it as the Holy Communion, and yet others as the Mass. Like baptism, this ordinance has been enshrined in the polity of nearly every branch of the Church. With most Christian bodies it far transcends baptism in significance. Baptists, on the contrary, have made more of the latter—due largely to severe persecutions in the early days because of their persistent practice of immersion, and their consequent refusal to " baptize " infants.

Attention is called to the uniformity with which Baptists denominate these two practices, " ordinances." By so doing they emphasize their conviction that these are empty of any and all sacramental implications. They at most *symbolize* experience, and in no sense communicate any sacramental grace. They have educative, but not saving value. Stated negatively, they are unnecessary to salvation, though potent in culturing the life in devotion to Christ.

At this point Baptists separate themselves sharply from all doctrines of a sacramentarian nature; and not infrequently from groups holding such views. This may seem unnecessary and regrettable, and yet it but illustrates the positive antipathy of this people to any suggestion that the source of salvation is other than Christ himself. He, and he only, is the mediator of salvation to men. This position places them at a pole wholly opposite to the Roman Catholic position, for instance, where the seven holy sacraments directly mediate saving grace, and appear to be the preeminent means of salvation.

Here we find the chief ground for the historic opposition of Baptists to the baptism of infants. They claim that the immediate implications of this practice are sacramental, and that implicit in it is the belief that in some mysterious way something necessary is done to the child when he is christened. Perhaps it begets the idea that without such baptism the child is " lost," but with it is " saved." Years ago, Lemuel Call Barnes, a notable leader among Baptists, said during an interdenominational missionary conference, " Infant baptism is the tap-root of Romanism." By this he was urging that with the Roman Catholic Church the seed of its whole sacramental system is planted in the act of sprinkling " holy " water on the child's head. This accords with the general Baptist view and constitutes the main reason for opposition to the practice. There are such other considerations as that there is no such baptism in the New Testament; that it makes too much of the ordinance, even as it expects too much of it, namely to save; and that it imposes upon the child that which belongs to his later years as a right— to be baptized or not, as he may himself elect.

Baptists, with very few exceptions, have been and are insistent on immersion as the one and only mode of baptism. As stated above, early persecution as a result of this insistence, and the necessity of defending their position all along, have conspired to give the ordinance what seems to many an undue emphasis and prominence. Other and valid reasons for insistence upon immersion only are not far to seek. It is the only mode known to the New Testament, and so the mode by which Jesus himself was baptized. It is the mode least likely to be used in the so-called " baptism of infants." As a symbol immersion is rich and full of meaning, in contrast to the poverty of other modes. The first of these reasons is strongly buttressed by present-day New Testament scholarship; the second no understanding person will care to deny; while the third not many will wish to dispute.

Let us consider this last-mentioned reason, namely, richness of symbol. It is an established fact that every enduring, human institution has created and nurtured some symbolism. Moreover, it seems quite clear that longevity is sustained by vital and dynamic symbolism.

# The Ordinances of the Churches

Why? Because symbols have power to teach and edify far beyond the capacity of words. If this be true the Baptist position seems secure: if the churches are to employ symbols let them be dynamic. Baptism by sprinkling or pouring can at most symbolize purification, and this is not a basic Christian concept. While on the contrary immersion symbolizes the deep and significant conversion experience; death to the old life of sin, burial of that old life and the rising to walk in newness of life with Christ. Or viewed somewhat differently, it symbolizes the death, burial and resurrection of our Lord, in whose experience we rest our hope of immortality (Col. 2:12; Gal. 3:27; Rom. 6:3-5). Baptism thus becomes a symbol of tremendous teaching potency, saying things to men that cannot otherwise be spoken. Words are most unequal to the task of setting forth either the experience of conversion or the hope of eternal life; the symbol of baptism is eloquent regarding both. Is it not an indisputable fact that Jesus inaugurated this Christian baptism for the very reason of its rich significance as a symbol and its consequent capacity to carry unspeakably precious truth across the centuries?

On casual thought, the Supper is the symbol of the Master's broken body and shed blood. But it is far more meaningful than that to the "initiated"—and symbols have little significance for others than the initiated. In deeper vein the Supper relates itself primarily to the disciple. For this disciple did not Christ die? Exactly so. Let us say then, that as baptism portrays the new life, so the Supper offers the only proper food for that life. If the new life is to prosper, it must feed upon its Lord. Christ himself puts it very poignantly when he instructs his disciples, "He that eateth my flesh and drinketh my blood, dwelleth in me, and I in him" (John 6:53-56). He is to be eaten! Not sacramentally; rather is it necessary that the disciple feed his mind on the Master's type of thinking; culture his soul by acquiring his Master's emotional life and by zealously aspiring to his Master's kind of conduct in all relationships, human and divine.

In the light of the foregoing, Baptists are always advocates of the logical sequence, discipleship first, then the ordinances. If baptism is a symbol of the new life, declaring it to the world, then that new life must antedate the ordinance. By the same token that new life must be existent prior to administration of that ordinance which symbolizes food therefor. Otherwise baptism proclaims that which does not exist, and the Supper offers food to that which is not yet born. In other words, as the ordinance of baptism precedes that of the Supper, so regeneration precedes both. Incidentally, herein lies another reason for the rejection of infant baptism, namely, that such baptism heralds the new life which, by nature of the case, does not yet exist.

Already we have indicated who is a candidate properly to receive the ordinances. It is the one who gives evidence of regeneration, who reveals in daily life a death to the old life of sin, who shows that the old life, being dead, has been surely buried, and who manifests that he now walks in newness of life, in a resurrected life, with his living Lord. The person who bears witness in his association with men to this regeneration may claim right to the baptismal declaration thereof. And having been baptized thus in "answer of a good conscience toward God" (1 Peter 3:21), or as a public testimony to the regenerate life within, he may then come to the table of his Lord, whereon is spread food, symbols of the feeding of the new life. Stated in historic Baptist phrase, the Supper is reserved for " the baptized believers "; and this assumes baptism by immersion. Out of this position came the polity of " close communion," discussed below.

The foregoing raises the question—in answer to which Baptists are by no means a unit—To whom do the ordinances belong, to the individual Christian, or to the local church as an institution? In general they have been conceived to belong to the institution. Hence baptism is the door of the church and the Lord's Supper a place of fellowship for those who have entered by that door. However, there have always been those Baptists who maintain that these ordinances were instituted for the individual, primarily, and not for the institution. Their position is that since the one ordinance is the symbol whereby the individual declares to the world his new life in Christ, and that since the second symbolizes the food by which that new life is to live, therefore these are vitally related to the individual Christian rather than to the church.

Viewing both positions, one must admit the truth in each; they are not in conflict, however. The institution is composed of individuals, and functions by and for them. Hence it seems a fair integration of both positions to say that the church accepts and maintains the ordinances for the edification of individuals. The institution persists, while individuals pass on; hence perpetuity of the ordinances presupposes the care of the churches; but such care is manifest in order that individuals may be ministered unto. As so often is the case, when the two positions are seen to be but two angles of the same truth they supplement each the other and negate the mistakes of extremes.

" Close communion " is a practice whereby only Baptists are invited to the Supper, in some rare cases only those of the one local church-membership. This item of polity, a practice becoming obsolete in widening circles of Baptists, rests back upon the institutional view of the ordinances—that they belong to the local church which may and does control the conditions of their celebration. With the infiltration of the other half of the truth, namely, that these ordinances are for the individual, though administered by the church, there comes a relaxing of the hand of the institution, and he who loves the Lord Jesus Christ, and feels the new life within, is bidden to the Lord's table. Such a practice, in contrast, is called " open communion."

It should be observed in passing that close communion is, in practical working, really *close baptism*. Only those may come to the table who are members of the church; and they are such by virtue of baptism by immersion. Hence a close communion practice excludes from the table all non-immersed, though they may be believers. The close communion polity, even though sectionally in vogue, has never been altogether congenial to Baptists themselves; it hardly comports with their doctrine of competency and their genius for soul liberty. This fact, we surmise, explains the quest rather far afield for buttressing reasons. For instance, this quest turned up the facts that the Passover in Egypt was a family institution, and also that our Lord instituted the Supper when none were present save the little family of the twelve disciples. And from these facts was deduced the amazing conclusion—therefore, only those should sit at the Lord's table who are members of the local church family. However, close communion is surely passing, weakened by the deep-flowing currents which unfailingly emerge in behalf of individual freedom and soul liberty. In the end, who may determine one's fitness to come to the table which the church spreads except oneself?

The institutional emphasis on the ordinances has caused Baptists to neglect their ministry to the aged, the sick, and other shut-ins. Administered only "by the church" has been narrowly interpreted to mean administered *only in the church*. Hence the carrying of the holy meal of remembrance to the shut-in—a beautiful ministry —has been almost wholly absent. This is to be regretted, and is chargeable to an overemphasis on institutionalism. This same emphasis has frowned upon spreading the table at out-of-door meetings, at conferences, conventions, and the like. Logic suggests the question why it should be thought proper to administer one of the two ordinances, namely, baptism, abroad, in any stream, lake, or pond, the while the other may not be moved from the church building? Perhaps necessity dictated the one practice and a fear of sacramental implications the other.

Who, in the Baptist polity, may minister these ordinances? There have been times when this was a perplexing question, particularly in the early days of the denomination. There was no apostolic succession, or anything remotely like it, to which they could appeal. Where, for example, might one turn who wanted to express his faith by baptism? To yield to a pedo-Baptist clergyman, though he were willing on occasion to immerse, would seem to endorse this clergyman's employment of other modes at other times. Not infrequently, therefore, ministers baptized themselves—"se-baptism"—and then baptized the men and women of their respective groups. Thus they sought to originate a new, spiritual succession, direct from Christ. When such a line of the properly baptized was thus established, the rights and privileges of administering the ordinances were passed forward through the service of ordination. By such ordination ministers are set apart for special ministerial functions within the churches, including the right to baptize and preside in serving the Lord's Supper.

This presupposes that the churches are the guardians of the ordinances, and as such bestow the right of administration upon whom they will. As indicated this is done uniformly by ordination; but not only so. Occasions and seasons come when no ordained minister is available, in which cases the church may, and frequently does, bestow upon a deacon or other member the right, temporarily, to officiate both at the pool and the table. In the case of baptism the suggested practice is limited to rare instances, whereas with the Supper it is as common as the other is rare. For this difference there is no logic, of course; but it has grown out of the practical experience of having appointed days for observing the latter ordinance, whereas baptism could wait until an ordained minister was available. These practices are further witnesses to the outworking of a non-sacramental evaluation of the ordinances.

An interesting observation as to the fluid nature of Baptist polity and its sensitivity to changing thought, or thought-emphasis, is seen today in the baptismal formula. There was a time when all were baptized in the name of "the Father, and of the Son, and of the Holy Ghost," as given at the end of Matthew's Gospel. Today one frequently hears, "in Jesus' name," "in the name of the Lord Jesus Christ," "into the discipleship of the Christ," and so on. The explanation? Primarily a gradual shift from a doctrinal to a life-emphasis, with the result that the Lord Jesus Christ himself comes to preside at the pool, instead of the *doctrine* of the Trinity; association with him in the enterprise of growing a princely life takes precedence over belief in an abstract doctrine, however true. Also there is the discovery that in that first book of the history of Christianity, the Acts of the Apostles, in no single recorded instance did those who administered the ordinance of baptism employ the trinitarian formula; there the practice was to emphasize regeneration in Christ (why the apostles, as viewed in Acts, do not honor the command of Matthew 28:19, we shall leave to New Testament scholarship to determine). And so today we witness the beginnings of a new, life-centered polity presiding when the ordinance of baptism is administered and the candidate is baptized *into the discipleship of the blessed Lord*. And that, of course, is the proper emphasis, namely, discipleship.

Baptist ministers have generally been at pains to administer the rite of baptism with a dignity that comports with its significance. The result is that a baptismal service makes a profound impression upon the serious-minded witness as well as upon the candidate. It is really a dramatic reenactment of the conversion experience. Thus baptism is an experience of sanctifying potency for the new-born in Christ and of vital devotional and didactic value to others. The writer bears witness to having baptized six young women, one Easter Sunday evening, before a congregation partly composed of a visiting group of the Masonic Fraternity. So beautifully did the young disciples conduct themselves, and so impressive was the service of their rededication to Christ and his way of living, that three strong men confessed later that they were moved to tears. If three made this admission, how many, may we judge, were equally moved, but did not confess loss of emotional control? We surmise Jesus knew exactly what he was about when he prescribed this telling symbol.

Far from uniform is practice as to preparation for baptism and church-membership. Churches, the major portion of whose gospel is baptism by immersion and who sing its glories both in and out of season, may be presumed adequately to prepare their candidates for the ordinance. Most Baptist churches, however, are advocates of a rich, full gospel of which baptism is a not too important part; it is the door to the church and the responsibilities of its membership. Increasingly, therefore, painstaking ministers are maintaining at different seasons of the church year a pastor's class into which they gather for several weeks' instruction those who contemplate church-membership. This is a wise and commendable practice. Some eschew the method because certain other bodies of Christians make so much of it. If it has proved good and wise in the experience of others, the more reason for adopting it—with such modification as may better meet Baptist needs. In such a class the pastor comes close to the candidates, especially young converts, when he may interpret to them with telling effect the deep meanings of the life in Christ and the rich significance of the church and its ordinances.

Other ministers and churches, however, are very lax in the matter of preparation; unpardonably so, let us plainly say. If these matters are so important as they aver, then let them be so treated. Greater care at the front door will spare the hinges of the rear exit. Baptist churches need to develop a polity at this point as effective and dignified as have their brethren, say, of the Episcopal and Lutheran communions.

We have stated above that the practice of close communion, once quite universal among Baptists, and still largely so in the Southern States, is really close baptism; only those may come to the table who are church-members by virtue of their being immersed believers. This polity has been long on the shift: the invitation to fellowship in the Lord's Supper having been first extended to all Baptists, then to members of immersing churches other than Baptist, and finally to " all who love the Lord Jesus Christ." This indicates, of course, that the basis of welcome to the sacred meal has moved, in the open communion churches, from baptism to discipleship, from a symbolic rite to the regenerate life symbolized thereby. That this is a most significant development, none will deny; and it seems better to comport with Baptist emphasis on regeneration rather than on a given rite.

The end of this development was not reached in the polity just indicated. Certain English Baptist churches long since began to practice mixed membership, that is, a membership composed of the immersed, those otherwise baptized, and those unbaptized by any method. Changing conditions in the States, particularly the over-churching of communities and the rapid rise of unchurched suburban areas (induced largely by the coming of excellent transportation facilities) have conspired to force open the doors of many American Baptist churches to non-immersed members from pedo-Baptist churches. The change has been going on quietly as a matter of necessity, if not always of desire. One or two partial studies of the extent of the open membership polity have been made, and these afford ground for the assertion that today it is the practice of hundreds of the churches, almost exclusively within the American Baptist Convention. Among these are found churches of all types, large and small, rural and urban.

The status of these members coming from non-immersing churches by letter is not yet uniformly fixed, hence may hardly be thought of as polity. Their status ranges all the way from loosely affiliated members, with limitation of rights and privileges, to membership in complete and regular standing.

The new life manifest in this old and knotted branch on the tree of Baptist polity is interesting, to say the least. It indicates that even here change and growth may be expected. It means a decided change in the hitherto uniform basis of membership; a change from the regenerate, *immersed* believer to the regenerate, *baptized* (of whatever mode) believer. This shift will be seen to be a lineal development of open communion, in that it lifts the chief emphasis off the rite of baptism and places it squarely upon the regenerate life.

In fairness to the increasing number of open membership Baptist churches we must set down their conviction that by this practice they in no wise relax their allegiance to the New Testament mode of baptism; for whenever they baptize, they immerse. They administer the rite in no other form, nor do they contemplate doing so. They are as positive immersionists as their fathers; they merely eschew their sectarianism by freely fellowshiping Christians to whom time has given many names. None, they aver, can contend fairly that Methodists, Presbyterians, Episcopalians, and others are on the whole less Christian than Baptists. Why then refuse to extend the hand of fellowship to these, since they show that they too have been with Jesus whom they know in a regenerate life? If the Lord has thus honored them and they him, who are we to refuse them membership with us, it is asked. Frankly, therefore, the churches referred to hold as central and cardinal *the Christ-kind of life* behind the rite of baptism, rather than the rite itself.

It is not in our purpose to praise or blame current developments in polity, but rather to record them. Such growth may be wise or unwise, only time and the experience of the churches will determine. One thing however there is about which we may be even dogmatic, namely, that such shifts in polity are entirely legitimate. The churches, being "competent," as they hold, may change their polity whenever and however they choose. They are soundly baptistic in so doing. By just such method the whole structure of polity as it exists today has grown. Baptist polity is like a tree whose changing twig and branch witness that it is alive.

### TOPICS FOR GROUP DISCUSSION

1. Define "ordinances," and indicate why Baptists use that term rather than "sacrament."

2. Resolved, that all churches should make baptism by immersion their one and only door.

3. Do the ordinances belong to the individual, or to the church? May they, then, be celebrated outside the church building?

4. What are the deep and fundamental facts of religious experience which lie back of the ordinances and give them real meaning?

5. Present the arguments for and against "open membership" in Baptist churches.

6. Distinguish between " regular membership," " open membership," and " mixed membership."

## Books Worth Consulting

Bromiley, G. W., *Baptism and the Anglican Reformers*. The Lutterworth Press, London, 1953.

Clark, Wayne C., *The Meaning of Church Membership*. The Judson Press, Philadelphia, 1950.

Cook, Henry, *What Baptists Stand For*. The Kingsgate Press, London, 1947.

Mullins, Edgar Y., *Baptist Beliefs*. The Judson Press, Philadelphia, 1925.

## Practical Suggestions

Aim to make your baptismal service comport in dignity and impressiveness with the great significance you believe baptism to have.

1. Make sure that every detail of the service as planned is attended to and in readiness. Let there be no loose ends, nothing left to chance.

2. Just before entering the pool meet your candidates in a group for final instructions. Suggest calm and composure. Rejoice with them in the great witness for Christ they are now to bear.

3. Enter the pool in beautiful self-composure, thus inspiring it in your candidates. Make every move meaningful, deliberate, and dignified. Be unhurried throughout. The pinning of a flower on each candidate will give time for gaining self-possession.

4. Having pronounced the baptismal formula you prefer, lower the candidate deliberately and quietly. As he is raised, step gracefully between him and the people,

and thus guide him to the exit unobserved. To this end the large flowing sleeve of the baptismal gown is a considerable aid.

Each item in the baptismal act should be rehearsed—in imagination—until the whole seems natural, graceful, and moving. This will make the difference between the ordinance worshipfully administered, and the ordinance made a mockery and a show.

## VIII

## THE CREATION OF A BAPTIST CHURCH

Every consideration of Baptist polity must begin with the doctrine of soul competency clearly in mind. It is, as we have consistently noted, the pole-star for the way Baptists are to go. This is preeminently true when we come to view the creation of a new local church.

Previously we have dealt with the matter of authority, authority for both individual and group. There arises here the question, By what authority is a Baptist church brought into being? The answer is close at hand: by the authority of the local group of regenerate, baptized believers in Christ. These individually being competent in all matters of religion, and in the exercise thereof, having crowned Christ as the lord of their lives, are collectively competent in all matters of church, even to the formation of a new church. Freely declaring Christ to be the one and only head of his church, the group becomes his immediate agent for the founding of a local church, as well as for carrying forward its ministry. In fact such a local group of regenerate believers is already a church; they are already a "called-out" group; the formal organization being necessary only for corporate life and action.

In this whole business only two parties are essentially concerned, the Saviour of men, who has a ministry for the world, and the saved, who acknowledge their responsibility to perform, to the best of their collective ability, that ministry in his name. To discharge this responsibility in an orderly way they must organize; in so doing they become a church in the institutional sense—at least Baptists so hold and teach. This may seem a heavy demand, namely, the promotion of the Master's work, to lay upon the hearts of a group of disciples; and so it is. But if they are competent then they must exercise such competency to the full in working out their own salvation and the salvation of the world. Competency does impose awful responsibility. But to run away from its implications is to invite spiritual death, and to be a party to injuring his cause who has no other plan for its promotion save by and through those who are fully his to give good and loyal service.

The newly created organization, in fulfilment of its high mission to carry forward the things which Jesus began to do and to teach, conceives its ministry under two phases: first, a ministry to its own members and constituency, and secondly, a ministry to the widest possible circle beyond. It feels an obligation not only to its own, but to all—for whom Christ died.

The first phase of this ministry is circumscribed, but intensive. It is to edify or build up the local membership and constituency. It is a ministry that aims at the direction of the growth of every man, woman and child toward Jesus Christ and his way of living; into his attitudes and interests; into his mind and manner; coming finally into large semblance of his passionate love and his fulness of life. This ministry is most profitably conceived in terms of education. The superlative method is to persuade each, by every chaste and becoming means, to fall in love with Him into whose likeness he would grow. This means joyous companionship, issuing in rich results.

The second phase of this ministry is extensive and expansive. The local church aims to extend its influence to the farthest bound, hence it becomes missionary in the fullest sense. It does not forget that it is Christ's agent, and that as such it must attempt to reach in its ministry as far as his interests run. With the mission of the church so conceived it is no accident that Baptist churches came early to be passionately missionary. Neither, it may be added, is their remarkable achievement in world-wide ministry a matter for marvel; they took seriously their divine charter, and God has blessed their labors accordingly.

Baptists are not unmindful that their view of the local church reposes upon them the larger weight of Kingdom responsibility. They acknowledge no ecclesiastical set-up, no hierarchy which may lift that responsibility. Therefore they are driven in the opposite direction, namely, to divine aid and guidance. The great Head of the churches is depended upon to strengthen and direct his agents, and it is confidently believed he will. Nothing is more pathetic than the disorder and chaos that result from a loss of this sense of the guidance of the living Christ, and a resort to the leadership of parties and politics.

This noble and ennobling thought of divine guidance, in practical affairs reveals unmistakable weakness. Perhaps it is the weakness, no more and no less than that which inheres in all democracies. For in such the people believe themselves divinely endowed and guided in self-government. The difficulty with "guidance" is that so many unwise and even silly people think themselves divinely directed to do those things which by common agreement of men would be pronounced positively evil. It is not stretching the plain truth to say that this folly has sometimes wrought the founding of another Baptist church against the higher interests of the Kingdom. Blame for such folly, shameful as it is, is mitigated by the remembrance that worldly wise hierarchies of one variety and another have sometimes also been guilty of like error.

Supposing that a certain group of regenerate men and women are desirous of bringing into being a Baptist church for their locality, how are they to proceed? Wisdom counsels that they call into conference near-by ministers and lay people with whom to confer about that which they have in mind. Particularly should they seek the thought of others as to the need and opportunity of the contemplated church. In an increasing number of localities there are organized permanent councils, and city mission societies whose Committee on Location of New Churches should be consulted as above suggested. Again, there are communities whose religious leaders have set up an interdenominational Committee on Comity, whose business it is to counsel as in the case before us. Those contemplating the organization of a new church, and desirous of moving in accordance with Kingdom welfare, will seek these available counsels as a check on their own felt guidance; for, is it not charitable to assume that other groups of Christians may also hear the guiding Voice? This idea of checking on guidance, happily on the increase in the polity of the churches, is not new among them. Baptists have long advocated, for example, that a young man's call to the Christian ministry should find undoubted echo in the church of which he is a member, the presumption being that if the Lord calls the young man, He will also call the church to send him forth with its blessing. Therefore logic urges those about to launch a new church enterprise to consult earnestly both the Lord and their neighbors—then do what seems the wise and Christian thing.

Should it be decided to go forward with organization, the place, day and hour therefor will be set, and a council composed of ministers and lay people from neighboring Baptist churches invited to be present for counsel, and participation if requested.[1] Where the churches of the Association affected have a council permanently organized, that is the body which should be invited, and whose president would normally call the meeting to order, if not actually preside by virtue of his office. Thus organized the meeting will proceed to adopt a name and articles of faith for the new church and to elect such officers as clerk, deacons, trustees, church school superintendent, and where possible call a minister. Thus simply created the new church is ready to begin its work. At some time during the ensuing year, likely at the time of the annual meeting of the Association, the young church will make formal application for " recognition " as a regularly constituted Baptist church. At that time, the churches assembled in annual conference—or semiannual, as the case may be—will ask for a review of proceedings hitherto, and to hear the covenant by which the members are bound and the articles of faith, or statements of doctrines, upon which they stand. Thus the church seeking entrance into the family of churches presents its case, and after full consideration the assembly votes whether or not to " recognize."

Should the vote be negative, the future of the infant church is precarious. The rejected group may disband—

---

[1] There are cases in which a group, ignoring both wisdom and fraternity, proceeds to organize itself into a church without seeking counsel of any other. When the organization is thus complete, " recognition " is sought.

usually the wiser procedure—or determine to carry on in an endeavor to demonstrate the worthiness of their request. Succeeding, they may at a later date again ask for recognition by sister churches.

The above is a case in illustration of the strategic importance of the Association, to be discussed in the next chapter. The churches of a given locality associated together constitute the keystone in the arch of Baptist polity. The Association claims no ecclesiastical authority, yet it may function with adequate control—the control of united opinion. Throughout the years these associational gatherings have not infrequently become the public forums wherein the chief elements of polity have been wrought out. Hence the decadence of the Association in many sections today may be fraught with ominous consequences. Does it mean that control is passing to State and national conventions, from home government to centralized government higher up? Such is the tendency of the times. Only experience can determine whether or not wisdom lies in that direction; if it does not, by the process of trial and error the churches will surely repeat their history and seek elsewhere the paths of health and wisdom. Such is the virtue of an unfixed, democratic polity; it may readily change to meet new situations.

When the newly constituted church has been duly accepted into the fellowship of the churches of the Association, articles of incorporation from the State are customarily sought. This is now possible in most if not all the States of the Union. Such articles enable the church legally to hold property and perform other acts legitimate to non-profit corporations.

In some sections, New England in particular, the laws

did not originally vest property rights in the church as such, but in the parish; a hangover from the Old World. The parish was organized as "the Society." Hence in many of the older Baptist churches of New England there yet exist side by side the church and the Society, the latter holding the property and bearing financial responsibility for the church and its work. This is a double-headed arrangement which in practice has not generally commended itself, and as a result it is rapidly disappearing. The States now enable the churches to incorporate and take over the property from the Society, which then disbands. This applies to other parts of the country where in early days this New England practice spread.

When a church has been recognized by sister churches, and duly incorporated by the State, it is considered fully competent in all matters pertaining to its conduct and ministry. Its authority comes from Christ, the supreme Head of his church, and it neither seeks nor accepts authority from any other source. Extreme exercise of this complete competency is seen when a church ordains its own minister or recovers a " lost ordinance," as in the case of baptism by immersion; John Smyth and other early founders baptized themselves (presumably at the instruction of the church), thus beginning a new apostolic succession of immersed believers. Not infrequently (as previously noted) in the absence of an ordained minister, a church requests one of its members to serve the Lord's Supper, or even perform the ordinance of baptism. These are cases of extremity, to be sure, but they illustrate the point that each church considers itself fully competent relative to these and all other matters of its life and work.

# The Creation of a Baptist Church

The practice referred to may produce astonishment in one unacquainted with such polity; it may seem to lead to all sorts of ill-advised acts; however, let such an one consider the facts: Here are thousands of churches, working in this wholly independent fashion, and yet they constitute a denomination than which few, if any, can show a more essential unity. Note, we do not say conformity —Baptist churches are very poor conformists, particularly if there is any semblance of coercion about. They are, however, splendid imitators, so that any method or procedure that works advantageously in one church or locality is sure to be carried elsewhere. In fact thus is polity grown. And thereby is vindicated a faith in men that holds, that, given freedom, they will gradually work their way to ground both solid and in common with others. Conformity by coercion is a very poor substitute for unity attained in a free quest.

## Topics for Group Discussion

1. By what line of reasoning can a group of baptized believers justify their organizing themselves into a Baptist church? By whose authority do they proceed?

2. Practical experience has evolved what items of polity as a check on the so-called " divine guidance " of this group? Do you approve of the permanent councils?

3. Resolved, that the principle of competency operative in the creation of new churches has worked lasting harm to Kingdom progress by overchurching many communities.

4. How does the Association significantly function in this field?

### Books Worth Consulting

Cook, Henry, *What Baptists Stand For*. The Kingsgate
 Press, London, 1947.

Early minutes of various churches. Consult church clerks
 or a denominational library.

Hiscox, Edward T., *The Standard Manual for Baptist
 Churches*. The Judson Press, Philadelphia, 1890.

### Practical Suggestions

Convert this class into a group desirous of organizing
itself into a new Baptist church. Let them choose a
name, proceed to seek wider advice, adopt proper credentials, elect necessary officers, call a minister, and finally
ask recognition by the Association.

The following forms are examples:

#### Letter Looking Toward Initial Council

(Place, date).

Rev. _____

_____

*Dear Sir and Brother:*

We the undersigned constitute a committee representing a group
of Baptists in the _____ vicinity, who are desirous of
organizing themselves into a Baptist church. Would you be so
kind as to counsel with us relative to this matter on __(date)__,
at ____(place)____? We would appreciate it moreover should
you ask one or more of your lay people to accompany you.

Yours in the Master's Service,

_____,

_____,

_____,

*Committee.*

P. S. This letter is being sent to others of the local Association.

# The Creation of a Baptist Church

Should the initial council, indicated in the foregoing letter, encourage the organization of the church, then the following letter should be addressed to each church in the local Association:

(Place, date.)

To THE _____ BAPTIST CHURCH,

_____

*Brethren:*

After prayerful consideration, and in accordance with the counsel of brethren from neighboring churches, it has been decided to create a Baptist church in _____. To help us in the matter of organization we request that you delegate your minister and one other member to meet with like members from sister churches in _____(place, date, hour, etc.)_____.

Yours in the Great Cause,

_____

In case the Association has a permanent council, then a letter should be addressed to its president requesting his advice as to proper procedure; such a council will have adopted some appropriate modes of action.

When the church is thoroughly organized, has called a minister, and has demonstrated the wisdom of its founding, then it should seek "recognition" by the Association. Where there exists a permanent council it should be allowed to direct procedure, but in the absence of such a council then the petitioning church makes known to— either or both—the moderator and the clerk of the Association its desire for recognition at the forthcoming associational meeting. This should be forwarded in writing, properly attested as an official action of the church, three months in advance of the meeting of the Association.

## IX

## THE ASSOCIATION OF CHURCHES

From the earliest years Baptist churches united hands in joint action. We have record of concerted action by five General Baptist churches in England, at least as early as 1624, fourteen years after the creation of what was evidently the first Baptist church. It is clear that such practice soon came to be common, the churches finding no inconsistency between local self-government and association for united effort. Within fifty years English Baptist churches had not only multiplied but were found definitely formed into Associations.

It cannot be forgotten that these free, dissenting churches arose out of bitter opposition, to say nothing of consistent persecution. Such conditions drove them together for mutual strengthening and protection, and that they might show a united front to their opponents. Moreover, they were insistent advocates of certain views—generally considered dangerously heretical—to propagate which concerted action was necessary. Local independency was an ideal which in actual practice had to yield sufficiently to make way for cooperation.

The first formal association of Baptist churches in America was on the part of those in and about Philadelphia, in both Pennsylvania and New Jersey, in the year 1707. They called their organization The Philadelphia Association. While the idea had come overseas from England, there were here also very definite urges toward interchurch fraternity. Considering the means of transportation of those days, the constituent churches were obviously scattered; and they were in need of keeping touch for acquaintance, for mutual edification, and for the propagation of the gospel as they understood it. For something like twenty years previous to 1707, the increasing number of churches of the Philadelphia area had been coming together annually and then semiannually in general meetings. These were informal gatherings for fellowship, inspiration, evangelism, and consideration of the many matters of concern. As the fellowship deepened into mutual confidence it was natural that they should venture a formal associational organization; further concrete evidence that the people were feeling their way forward, working out their polity as they went along.

With the example of sister churches in England and the nearer example of the Philadelphia Association, the associational idea spread with the rapid multiplication of the churches, North, South, and West, until it became the uniform polity. The area of these associations varied, dependent upon the number and location of the churches. The Philadelphia situation was typical; here associational bounds crossed the Delaware River. Associational lines were and are redrawn from time to time as a result of divisive opinion or to meet changing conditions. To use Philadelphia as illustration again, that Association not only does not now include any New Jersey churches, but has itself known shifting boundaries and today stands divided into a smaller territory denominated The Philadelphia Association and a larger, the North Philadelphia Association. With the passing years, however, in many States associational boundaries tend to coincide with those of the county.

The principle involved in the Association is significant. It is not considered an abridgment of local independency or local autonomy, but rather an enlargement thereof. The former might easily become isolation and strangulation, whereas the latter gives outlet for the strength and wisdom generated in the local group. So considered, the associational principle becomes, next to independency, the most potent single development in Baptist polity. Its rise seems providential; it operated for nearly three hundred years preparing the churches for our era of large-scale cooperation. Aside from the closest cooperation on the part of all the churches, the great world-wide enterprises could neither have come into being nor have moved forward to meet the challenge of the recurring years. Viewed in the light of history, it is not too much to believe that the living and directing Head of the churches inspired and nurtured the associational idea among the people. It seems to be too freighted with wisdom to be wholly of human origin.

It would be overstating the case to suggest that the two ideas, independency and cooperation, have never been in conflict. The technique for holding the two in harmonious wedlock has been slowly and painfully worked out through these generations. It has been a development attended by " growing-pains." Trial and error, debate, controversy, and compromise are all written in the pages of the years, pages eloquent of the cohesive power of the churches. Schism has sometimes walked abroad, but rarely has it been able to do its baneful work; the assured guidance of the many has been accepted by the few for the sake of the common cause.

Otherwise apprehended the problem of the Baptist churches is identical with that of centralization and decentralization in government. The puzzle is to find a proper balance between local and federal governments; a fully

satisfactory solution for which, needless to say, has not
yet been found. And by the very nature of the case
can never be found. We live in a changing world wherein
new situations continually arise demanding adjustments.
A satisfactory balance between the two today would
surely be found inadequate for tomorrow. The only
wise policy, therefore, is that of constant and wise
readjustment; a policy by the law of which men grow
in ability to govern themselves.

Among the churches, as in the realm of politics, there
are always those who not only hope for, but demand,
some fixed arrangement by which the respective spheres
of local church and denominational interests are permanently established. Such a hope is an idle dream, for only
in a fixed world can wisdom find a fixed polity. It is far
more challenging to see ourselves in a changing world
which constantly stabs us awake with the necessity of
facing new situations. Baptists may well thank God that
they have been led to maintain a fluid polity, for wherever polity sets, mentality congeals. Spiritual death follows such stagnation. The associational principle, as developed among this people from the beginning, brings
them to two elemental "musts"—they must maintain
the independency of the local church, and they must
cooperate with sister churches in the wider Kingdom enterprise. To fail in either becomes a cardinal apostasy
to Baptist faith and practice.

It is no exaggeration to say, as before affirmed, that
the Association is the keystone in the arch of Baptist
polity. From the earliest days, the associational gatherings were given to conference and the consideration of
every conceivable moral and religious problem that concerned either individual or church. Problems of right

conduct, correct teaching, proper interpretation of Scripture, and church polity were all brought to the floor or platform of the meeting for discussion. On the associational anvil of public discussion were forged those counsels which have guided the Baptists in making their contribution to an enriched Christianity and an expanding kingdom of God. One may marvel that out of such a method there has come so commendable a world-wide unity among twenty million people. It argues strongly for the modest belief that God has a stake in this democratically minded group of Christians; and that therefore they have had his watch-care. Let us hasten to add, however, that Baptists have no disposition to claim divine favor above other groups of brethren in Christ; they merely voice history's vindication of their emphasis.

In a previous chapter we have cited the decline of the Association; in wide areas it has only a name to live. We have raised the question if this is not an ominous fact. If the Association is the keystone, does its decline not foretell the weakening of the arch? One might so conceive it, though such a position is not necessary. Perhaps it has performed its mission. It may be that other items of polity have arisen to carry forward the work it so splendidly began.

There is no *ex cathedra* reason why the Association should abide, any more than there is such a reason why it should first have arisen. It came into being to meet a need; there is no cause for its remaining an item of polity unless it continues to meet that or some other vital need. A vermiform appendix in polity is a fit subject for removal, quite as certainly as one in a human body. The useless is never very inspiring. But is the Association no longer useful?

# The Association of Churches

Whether or not they are valid reasons, one need not seek afar to find those which account for the sickly pallor which is cast over the Association. First of all, the felt need for fellowship has been greatly lessened; increase of population and improved facilities of transportation have served to cast each of us into the midst of the crowd. Our impulsive tendency is no longer to seek folks, but rather to run away from them. For mere fellowship Baptists no longer *need* the associational gathering. In the second place, not only the main lines of the polity but largely the details also have already been wrought. Rarely do living issues in this realm come up for consideration; here the Associations have finished their work for the most part. A discussion that matters much on an associational platform today would be novel indeed. Then there have arisen State and national associations, or " conventions," and these have tended to overshadow the Association. These larger gatherings are the present-day debating societies where polity is in the making. Along with these has come to Baptists a sense of denomination; it is difficult longer to think in terms of the smaller unit which has come to be comparatively insignificant. And finally, Baptists seem to have lost largely their sense of a specific mission; and this is not well for any people.

Men cannot, and should not, wish to turn backward the wheels of time. Nevertheless the author laments the declining influence of the Associations, and ventures the hope that their former glory may return. It is not good for the churches when the center of influence and control moves too far from the home base. Baptists must not lessen their denominational and interdenominational cooperation, but they ought to find a way to bring every vital issue down for local consideration. Overcentralization is as undesirable as too great decentralization. The present ailment of the Association is symptomatic of the former. Baptists may no longer need the associational meeting merely for human fellowship, but the suggestion is advanced that they never more than now needed a fellowship around and concerning their great common task. And as for their polity it may be already quite grown-up, and units larger than the Association may be able to direct future growth. Still, the people in that unit nearer home need the opportunity to wrestle with and determine such issues. The multitudes who compose the churches must be educated concerning and inspired for the worldwide task; but they can never be so edified by State and national conventions. The logical educative and inspirational unit is the Association, and this day weakens its influence at the peril of a whole ministry to the world.

The " sense of denomination " that has come to Baptists is gratifying. To be a soldier in an army of twenty million gives one a feeling of strength, confidence, and pride. The rise of such a sense of solidarity among the thousands of independent churches is wholesome. The task before them is to nurture and conserve all this, meanwhile keeping high above the threshold of vitality the local church and its association with neighboring churches. The denominational consciousness gives vision and power. While church and Association grow, the people may see the vision and do something worth while about it.

The chief cause of depression in associational life, as stated above, is to be found in the loss of a conviction that the Baptist churches have a definite and peculiar mission. A Baptist church is just another church. For any denomination to lose that great incentive is serious and may become calamitous. One may say this, meanwhile deprecating the extremes to which such sense of mission has not infrequently led—even the follies and sins of rampant sectarianism. The day for such to go unrebuked is passed. Well beyond these, however, the Baptist churches have yet a peculiar work to perform; as we profoundly believe every great denomination has. Contributions from each make a rich and full presentation of the whole truth as it is in Jesus Christ.

What is the unfinished task of Baptists? In their three hundred and fifty years they have won many battles: freedom of conscience, separation of church and state, freedom of speech and press, and many others; but their battle for the recognition of the full competency of the human soul in matters of religion has not yet issued in victory. Strong sectors of the Christian world are still held by those who consider that principle mischievous and spurious, while the non-Christian world has not even dreamed of the power in that concept to liberate its millions bound by priestcraft and ignorance. Never was the need for the Baptist witness greater, nor the challenge more stirring. To see that need and hear that call would cure most of the petty ills that vex the denomination to-day. And it would contribute to a revival of the local Association, by bringing to Baptists a praiseworthy sense of a peculiar mission.

In this connection let it be noted that a strange overemphasis has given many non-Baptists the idea that Baptist churches exist chiefly to advocate baptism by immersion. The fact is, that is little more than a non-essential raised into undue prominence by controversy. Indeed, Baptists historically have minimized the rite by robbing it of all its sacramentalism and reducing it to a mere symbol. Baptists have clung to immersion as the proper mode of baptism for two chief reasons; first, because it is a practical buttress to soul competency—infants, unable to exercise competency, are not likely to be immersed—and, secondly, because it is the New Testament mode. A third reason seems to us even more potent, namely, that if the church is to employ symbolism, let it be that which is richest and fullest in meaning. Immersion meets this requirement.

The rank and file of the people in the churches need to be educated concerning these cardinal tenets of the Baptists; and the associational gathering is the place to do it. The conclusion of the whole matter is that the Association ought to remain pivotal in Baptist polity. Few changes in emphasis would result more profitably than a five-year moratorium on centralization of influence, with increasing attention to decentralization in favor of the Association. Current denominational weakness is proportionate to associational decadence.

A more recent outgrowth of associational life, in metropolitan areas, is the city mission society. From the outset, the churches united through the Association to promote missionary and evangelistic work, particularly within associational confines. In time, not a few associations became largely or wholly urban, and hence were faced with missionary and evangelistic opportunities to meet which their loose organization was unequal. This need called into being the metropolitan missionary society, whose area of operation is generally coterminous with that of an Association. The relationship between the two is being wrought in the school of experience, hence a new bit of Baptist polity is in the making. The virtue of the new organization lies mostly in specialization, under the direction of an executive secretary and his staff; it can say,

# The Association of Churches

"This one thing I do," which the associated churches could not. So efficiently have these city mission societies vindicated their existence that they have been accepted as affiliating organizations of the American Baptist Convention. Lack of any large number of congested metropolitan areas in the territory of the Southern Baptist Convention has delayed, for Southern Baptists, the critical city situations of the North.

## Topics for Group Discussion

1. The churches lifted anchor and sailed away from independency when they began to form themselves into Associations. Yes or no?
2. Polity as we know it was fashioned largely in the crucible of public debate at associational meetings. True or false?
3. Resolved, that authority may be more wisely vested in the Association than in the local church.
4. How solve the problem of centralization of authority so necessary to efficiency, and local autonomy so essential to education of the people?
5. Let the Association be scrapped as a bit of outworn and useless machinery. Debate the proposition.

## Books Worth Consulting

Early minutes of various associations. Consult clerks or denominational libraries.

Torbet, Robert G., *A History of the Baptists.* The Judson Press, Philadelphia, 1950; revised 1955.

Vedder, Henry C., *A Short History of the Baptists.* The American Baptist Publication Society, Philadelphia, 1907.

### PRACTICAL SUGGESTIONS

Study your local situation to ascertain what your Association is actually doing to make itself a real force for advancing the Kingdom in its territory. Discover if it is as vital as formerly; what are the causes in case it has lost potency and prestige; whether or not it should be revitalized, and if so, how.

In the course of your study, and particularly if it seems to lead you to undertake rejuvenation, it will be well to keep in mind that one of the most significant services the Association of yesterday performed was to provide a public forum on any and all issues of common concern to the churches. The wide spheres of doctrine, polity, program, and life all furnished their annual quota of items for debate at the associational gatherings. Thus the Association was a forceful factor in the education of its constituency.

There is a need today for that sort of thing—a forum where the people may gather to discuss matters of interest to church, denomination, and Kingdom. Thinking and planning were formerly done by the people; very essential functions which have gradually been delegated to headquarters' staffs; with the inevitable result of loss of interest locally. The need today is to bring policies, programs and the like, which are being proposed, back to the local churches for discussion and final judgment. There is, perhaps, overmuch handing-down and talking-down at associational meetings of matters already finished and fixed.

Work out a program for your Association which shall constitute, not a series of addresses by denominational leaders, but a series of debates and discussions on vital issues proposed by those leaders. Choose to lead these discussions honored ministers and lay people known for their fair and judicial minds (omit the known controversialist!), and give ample opportunity for full and free discussion " from the floor." Begin modestly, bringing up for consideration the great constructive issues. In time you may be able to revive the custom of our fathers, who discussed even controverted matters with calm and fairness.

# X

## STATE AND NATIONAL CONVENTIONS

The structural life of the Baptists as a denomination pyramids in symmetrical fashion. A broad base is laid in the multitude of local churches; superimposed is the lesser number of associations; these are in turn surmounted by a smaller number of state conventions; which are overarched by the so-called national conventions; the apex being reached in the Baptist World Alliance. A graph of this organizational structure would be geometrically regular, rising in an orderly way from base to apex.

Nevertheless, the growth of this pyramid has been far from orderly. Churches have not united into associations, associations into state or district conventions, and these into "national" groupings. For instance, state conventions have frequently antedated the formation of certain associations within convention territory; just as the Triennial Convention, embracing North and South, was organized in 1814 in advance of most, if not all, the state conventions later carved from its territory.

Even so, the denominational organization and polity have arrived finally at orderliness, and for sake of clearness of thought we may proceed in orderly fashion to the study of the completed pyramid. Hence from the association we pass on to state, national, and world conventions.

Associations, as we have noted, sprang into being in response to needs felt by the churches. Likewise it was need that produced the larger units now under consideration. Just as isolated churches were inadequate to the needs surrounding them, so there were opportunities in " distant parts " which could not be entered into save by wider organizational life. This latter consideration is the creative force responsible for State and national organizations, with their characteristic polities.

If it was the urge to fellowship and mutual counsel that created the Associations, it was the missionary passion that made the State convention a necessity. The Associations were scattered and bore the inherent weaknesses of decentralization in the presence of State-wide missionary opportunities, to meet which, united action must be achieved. This need dictated an organization not only wider in its scope of operation, but so closely knit as to be effective. Even so, it remained from the outset the *agency of the churches,* whatever the basis of representation in its make-up.

Beginning as a society for the propagation of the gospel in " distant parts "—the State bounds, and sometimes beyond—the State convention has had a phenomenal organizational development and a greatly enlarged sphere of influence. It has come to be the " holding corporation " for the denomination within the respective States. It still keeps to its primary missionary function by giving aid and nurture to weak churches, by the planting of new churches, and by establishing Christian centers and other mission projects in congested urban sections and among Newer American groups. But in addition, it has come to safeguard the whole denominational interest within the State borders; it promotes missionary education, stimulates and lifts to the best-known standards the Sunday schools; it fosters institutions of higher learning; educates concerning, and collects the funds for, the national convention and its cooperating organizations; and by the maintenance of a considerable staff of workers encourages and nurtures all of the Baptist interests within its domain.

The State convention is a delegated body representative of churches and associations, varying as each such convention determines. It holds at least one meeting annually, and thus in general convention any matter of concern to the churches, the State work, or the denomination may come up for public consideration. These annual convocations are from two to four days in duration. For the guidance of their deliberations an outline program is prepared in advance by a committee appointed for the purpose. The convention retains the right, however, to delete from or add to the proposed program.

The convention operates between annual meetings through a board of managers, of its own choosing. This board employs an executive secretary and such further staff as need and funds dictate, and through these promotes the work of the convention. The annual report of the board to the convention—prepared by the executive secretary—naturally advances the major items which elicit the consideration of the assembled delegates. In open convention, therefore, items of work, program and policy are determined. Such become binding upon board and executive secretary, but not upon the individual churches. In other words, the convention is advisory only, in no sense legislative. Its findings are merely recommendations to the churches, which, however, with few exceptions, consider them morally binding, since each church is a constituent member of the general body.

Looking denominationward, the State convention is most significant; it is the prime conservator of denominational interests. So significant is it in the total scheme of Baptist polity (we are writing particularly of Baptists in the United States), that some authorities consider it central. While we do not agree, we shall refrain from " entering the lists " in behalf of the Association. In fact, considering the trend toward centralization—that is, toward strong denominationalism—during the last quarter of a century in particular, the State convention has played an increasingly significant rôle; it has overshadowed the influence of the Association. Whether this is a wise development only time may determine; and we are perfectly willing to leave the matter to that court of final appeal. However, our judgment is that Baptist genius sinks its roots in and draws its power from the local church, and that since the State convention has a tendency to look in the other direction it carries within itself great weaknesses. If it can discover how effectively to stand at the middle and look both ways (a difficult feat), it will deserve immortality—and have it! For Baptists must effect, at one and the same time, both local *and* denominational strength, passion and virility.

The American Baptist Convention, in recognition of the place and influence of the State convention, has given it the status of " affiliating organization." As such it plays the rôle of unofficial observer to the larger body, yet it exercises no little power in the shaping of policy and the creation of program. It is in the budget of the national convention, as are also the various national societies— termed " cooperating organizations "—and along with these forms the dominant influence in the life and work of the convention.

Regardless of the position held by the State convention in the arch of Baptist polity, it remains a creation and agent of the churches. It is of the churches, by the churches, and for the churches; the instrument by means of which they present a united front to the problems they meet within their respective States. The temper of the convention is to lead the churches in an effective expression of their faith and life, and in no sense to lord it over any local group. It constitutes one of the finest illustrations of the adage, " In union there is strength," known to modern church life.

But the proper use of strength is a problem for the strong. The power of a great denomination is not to be lightly treated; power challenges the spirit of Christian leaders quite as much as the power of a mighty nation its chief executive. In either case such power should be considered a sacred trust, to be used only for the extension of the kingdom of God. This searching consideration, happily, is responsible for not a few experiments in federation of local churches, and in interdenominational comity within designated districts. In illustration, we may cite the many experiments in federation in New England and those in comity in the Montana, Utah, and Idaho Conventions.

In these enlightened days it is a burden to record these cooperative moves as " sporadic "; they should be the rule and not the exception. The employment of denominational power and prestige to further the sins of sectarianism, and a divisive Protestantism, is an abuse of power. Where such is the policy, the churches must be silent about " economic imperialism," and similar manifestations of unrighteousness, for super-denominationalism is of the same piece. Sensitive Baptist leaders are deeply conscious of the truth of this contention, but how to extricate conventions and churches therefrom is a

sizable and baffling problem. It seems clear that little
can be done until a new spirit—a spirit of genuine Kingdom interest—springs up in all the denominations concerned. The problem is akin, for intricacy and stubborn-
ness, to that of international disarmament; all profess to
desire it, but few are willing to make any sacrifice to attain it. But the thing must be done, for the day of competing conventions, with the consequent waste of sacred
funds, approaches the sunset hour. In what directions
the polity of cooperation will develop it is too early to predict, but unless we greatly mistake the temper which is
to dominate the next century—a century whose generations will carry over little of the contentions and controversial spirit that gave us sectarianism—a polity adequate
thereto is in the womb of tomorrow. Should Baptists
seize the banner of widening cooperation, as four generations ago they seized the banner of foreign missions, another glorious chapter of their history would be written.
The need of the hour is another Adoniram Judson and
another Luther Rice with sufficient vision and daring to
break the chains that bind, and to leap the barriers set
by an inherited, non-cooperative denominationalism.

We have already made reference to the denomination,
implying organization and polity operative in areas wider
than the State convention. As local needs early created
the Associations, and widening missionary opportunities
brought into being State organizations, so, and for like
reason, came the more inclusive national convention. The
first such organization among Baptists of the United
States was " The General Convention of the Baptist Denomination in the United States for Foreign Missions."
It was created in 1814, in the city of Philadelphia. By
virtue of its meeting every three years it came generally

to be called " The Triennial Convention." As the legal name implied—and the significant date of organization would lead the informed to surmise—the creative urge for this general convention was the foreign mission enterprise. The Judsons had reached Burma in 1813, and Luther Rice returning had been the moving spirit in arousing Baptists to a sense of their world-wide opportunity and responsibility. To enter this open door, united action was necessary; hence the Triennial Convention.

Under its banner Baptists of the North and South marched on to victory after victory in the great work to which they had set hand and heart. Then came the controversy over slavery, so violent and deep-rooted that it could not be kept out of denominational work. For instance, the question arose as to whether or not the foreign mission board should appoint a slave-owner for service abroad. The decision was negative and the die was cast. In 1844 there came a split in the denomination which meant death to the Triennial Convention; to the sorrow of the leaders of both North and South. All were resolved, however, that the missionary enterprise should not suffer; hence each section promptly worked out its own polity for conserving and forwarding that movement.

Consequently the Southern Baptist Convention was organized during the following year, 1845, in the city of Augusta, Georgia. It was born of the missionary passion and for its fullest expression has labored throughout the years. It has effectively nurtured, directed, and administered a splendid world-wide missionary work, and has also solidified the Baptists of the Southland in support of a complex and effective ministry in other lines of work, missionary, educational, philanthropic, and publication. As elsewhere noted, the sense of denomination has grown very strong, a testimony to the superlative effectiveness of the Southern Convention.

What of the local church in this South-wide set-up? This question of the local church, source of authority among Baptists, always arises. The constitution adopted by the Southern Convention made clear the independence of the churches:

It shall be the design of the Convention to promote foreign and domestic missions, and other important objects connected with the Redeemer's Kingdom, and to combine for this purpose such portions of the Baptist denomination in the United States as may desire a general organization for Christian benevolence, which shall fully respect the independence and equal rights of the churches.

Moving among the churches one hears no complaint of denominational overlordship. All feel their independence and practise it. There is a decided pride in the denomination of which they are a part; a feeling worthy of commendation, except where pride begets a local policy of " do nothing "—or as near nothing as possible.

The basis of representation in the Southern Convention, from 1888 up to 1931, is most interesting because somewhat unusual. The churches as such had no representation, whereas individuals and Associations did have. This indicates a denominationward point of view and trend, a movement toward centralization rather than decentralization. The major emphasis was on cooperation through an organic union of the various denominational agencies. The result is that the Baptists of the Southland have a very strong denominational consciousness, and the consequent solidarity of forces which any people might covet who seek a large cooperation—barring of course the very evident danger of sectarianism. The article in the Constitution to which we refer, after the form given it in 1904, reads as follows:

The Convention shall consist, (1) of brethren who contribute funds, or are delegated by Baptist bodies contributing funds for the regular work of the Convention, on the basis of one delegate for every two hundred and fifty dollars actually paid into the treasuries of the Boards during the fiscal year ending the thirtieth day of April next preceding the meeting of the Convention; (2) of one representative from each of the District Associations which cooperate with this Convention, provided that such representative be formally elected at the annual meeting of his District Association, and his election certified to the Secretaries of the Convention, either in writing or by copy of the printed minutes.

However, at the session of the Convention held in Birmingham, Alabama, in May, 1931, this basis of membership was very radically changed by a rewriting of the Constitution relative to delegates or messengers. It strongly reaffirms the historic Baptist emphasis on the significance of the local church. In other words, the change looks toward decentralization in the multitude of churches, each of which is to have one representative in the Convention, however small its gift to the denominational enterprise. In all probability this will have no practical effect upon the efficiency of the denomination, yet it is a symptom that reveals the determination of the churches to keep control in their own hands.

The Convention shall consist of messengers who are members of missionary Baptist churches cooperating with the Southern Baptist Convention on the basis of one messenger for every church contributing to the work of the Convention and one additional messenger for every $250 actually paid to the work of the Convention during the calendar year preceding the annual meeting of the Convention, such messengers to be appointed to the Convention by the churches and certified by the churches to the Convention, provided no church shall be entitled to more than ten messengers.

## State and National Conventions

The work of the Convention is carried on through boards of managers elected by the Convention. From these are appointed such executive officers as the work in hand demands, who formulate policy and program.

The Convention shall have as many Boards as, in its judgment, may be necessary for carrying out the benevolent objects it may determine to promote. Each of these Boards shall consist of eighteen members residing at or near the locality of the Board, and of one member for each cooperating State and the District of Columbia. The members of the Boards shall be divided into three groups as nearly equal as possible, one group to be elected each year and to serve three years. The President of the Board and the local members shall constitute the executive committee of the Board and fifteen members shall constitute a quorum of the full Board for the transaction of business. Each Board shall elect a President, Recording Secretary, Treasurer, Auditor, Executive Secretary who may be named its Treasurer if deemed advisable, additional Secretaries and such other officers and employees as it may deem necessary for the efficient conduct of its work and business. The compensation of its officers and employees shall be fixed by each Board, but no salaried officer or employee of any Board may be a member thereof. To each Board shall be committed, during the recess of the Convention, the entire management of all the affairs relative to the objects with whose interests it shall be charged; all of which management shall be in strict accordance with the constitutional provisions adopted by this Convention, and such other instructions as may be given from time to time. Each Board shall be authorized to enact its own By-laws.

*(From the Constitution as printed in 1934.)*

Following the dissolution of the Triennial Convention in 1844, Northern Baptists moved in a different direction, and hence evolved a different polity. Independent boards, or societies, were created, each to care for some specific phase of the work of all the churches. From the point of view of polity there was no denomination; there was, however, a large measure of united action. Along such lines the work developed for more than sixty years, so that by the dawn of the new century there were working throughout the Northern States, more or less independently, the American Baptist Foreign Mission Society, and its auxiliary, the Woman's American Baptist Foreign Mission Society; The American Baptist Home Mission Society, and its auxiliary, the Woman's American Baptist Home Mission Society; and The American Baptist Publication Society.

These came together annually for what appeared to be a convention, but was popularly known as " the May Meetings." At some designated place and time all these national societies—so-called—came together to hold, in turn, their respective annual meetings. Members of the churches congregated—whoever wished—to enjoy the feast of information and inspiration. Thus, the program of " the May Meetings " lacked unity or coherence in proportion as these virtues were absent in the societies.

These independent societies had more than amply justified their existence during the years. In a sense their very successes cost them independence. Each had extended its influence among the churches throughout the North, so that there arose overlapping and overcrowding, with their attendant misunderstanding and conflict. Moreover, each came to the churches to educate and to solicit funds, with certain undesirable results. In the first place, the local church had its interests divided among many organizations, so many that some churches solved the problem by abjuring interest in certain of them, or all. In the second place, the churches often seemed to be purely promotion agencies for the various societies; no time or strength being left for worship, education and edification.

## State and National Conventions

Consequently agitation grew for denominational unity, until finally the Northern Baptist Convention was organized, in 1907, in Washington, District of Columbia. At the outset the Convention structure was weak. The various societies were *asked* to become cooperating bodies of the Convention, but fearing the loss of independent action their response was hesitant. Some did not come into the new venture at once and those which did were exceedingly jealous of their rights. Fears were finally dispelled and general opinion pressed all to come into the cooperative enterprise. Since 1910 there has been a rapid development denominationward. Polity, however, is still in the making.

The most significant move toward centralization was the creation of the General Board of Missionary Cooperation; hastened by World War days and experiences that revealed the value of close coordination and cooperation. This board, in 1924, shortened to the Board of Missionary Cooperation, was designed to become the promotion and collection agency throughout the denomination for all the cooperating societies. The first task to which it set its hand, really the task that called it into being, was the New World Movement of 1919-1920. With this it succeeded notably; and later it in general justified its existence. However, not a few vexing problems of polity continue. Many Baptists are always fearful of centralization; societies long independent do not work comfortably under arrangements of cooperation; and some " view with alarm " overhead costs. But general agreement prevails among the leaders that they must forge a denominational organization and polity under which each cooperating society may find a way happily and effectively to work for the common or Kingdom good. Northern Baptists did not embark upon the denominational highway until the time was overripe, and the chances of retreat now are very slight. Progress, surely, lies straight ahead.

The continuous effort to develop a feasible organizational structure may be illustrated by the studies and decisions of the Convention in that area over a number of years. In 1933, the Convention, meeting in Washington, D. C., created a " representative Commission of Fifteen " to study the entire structure of the Convention and make a report at the next annual meeting. Accordingly, at the annual meeting of the Convention in Rochester, in 1934, a number of noteworthy changes were proposed. From the report of this Commission of Fifteen, we print three articles which have significance to polity.

### I. THE AUTHORIZATION OF THE COMMISSION

The Northern Baptist Convention at its annual session in the city of Washington in May, 1933, authorized by resolution the appointment of a " representative Commission of Fifteen," to which were referred " all recommendations from committees or individuals," whether made at the time of the Convention or later, " having to do with the organization or reorganization of the Convention or of any of its participating organizations." It was instructed to " give proper consideration in its recommendations to the principles of

(a) Historic Baptist democracy.
(b) An equitable basis of representation.
(c) Cooperation rather than centralization."

### II. GENERAL STATEMENT OF THE TASK

Among the items of major importance referred to this Commission were:

1. The question of annual or biennial sessions of the Convention.

2. Rotation in the membership of the boards of the Convention and of cooperating societies.

3. The consolidation of the mission societies.

4. The unification of the educational activities of the denomination.

5. Methods of raising denominational moneys.

6. Revision of the By-laws of the Convention.

### III. GUIDING PRINCIPLES

Since the local church is the most important factor of organization in our Convention, our recommendations have been made with both its welfare and responsibility in mind. We have steadily sought to achieve simplicity, economy and democracy of representation. We have, at the same time, tried to avoid the evils caused by the centralization of authority. We have believed that functions rather than the preservation of existing societies should determine the form of our denominational organization.

As a result of the studies made by the Commission of Fifteen, certain far-reaching changes in the organizational structure of the denomination were made. For the Board of Missionary Cooperation and its dependent machinery there was substituted a General Council and a series of subordinate " subsidiary councils ": the Council on World Evangelism, the Council on Christian Education, and the Council on Finance and Promotion. The General Council became the *ad interim* convention. It was composed of the officers of the Convention together with thirty other members, of whom groups of ten were to be elected annually, to serve for a period of three years.

A policy which operated against fixity of membership and control by any given section of the country was seen in the composition of the General Council, whose members were elected for a term of three years, and might not be re-elected for a third term until one year out of office had elapsed. Moreover, the Council at all times was required to have among its members at least four from each of three Convention areas: the Eastern, Central, and Western, respectively.

However, that which nominally suffices for one period often fails to meet the needs of a new day. A healthy discontent with the organization of the denomination persisted, and this led to further rethinking. In the years that followed, the position of general secretary was established. In 1956, at Seattle, the Convention provided for a strong General Council, two subsidiary councils; namely, the Council on Missionary Cooperation, and the Council on Christian Social Progress, as well as a number of boards and committees. It strengthened the General Council (which, by that time, consisted of thirty-six, instead of thirty, elected members), giving it wider powers and relating it more closely to the Council on Missionary Cooperation by requiring that an associate general secretary of the General Council be the Executive Secretary of the Council on Missionary Cooperation. Another innovation made at this time was the creation of the Staff Committee on Program Coordination, whose duty became that of considering the programs proposed by various organizations related to the Convention, initiating programs of its own, and advising the General Council and the respective organizations related to the Convention of its conclusions and recommendations.

These are but illustrations of the manner in which the Convention constantly seems to move. There is to be seen in them a development toward a closely knit and more perfect unity of its many functioning parts. To the student of polity two items of surpassing interest emerge from such changes: on the one hand, the fact that polity is alive and still in the making; on the other, the swinging back and forth of the pendulum indicating the drift toward either centralization or decentralization of the power of the Convention.

three groups have varied widely, their polity has passed through the stages of growth marked by associations; then larger combinations of churches within wider districts such as States and Provinces; and finally into more general conventions. In England this movement has culminated in the Baptist Union for Great Britain and Ireland, incorporated in 1890. In Canada, a solidarity was achieved in 1944 by the union of the three existing conventions in the Baptist Federation of Canada. In each case the larger and culminating body aims to unite into one effective and efficient whole all of the existing independent missionary and philanthropic societies and organizations.

In conclusion, this pertinent observation. No phase of polity in Baptist churches seems ever to have been adopted merely for the sake of uniformity, or in order to be fully up to date in terms of organization and method. There has been without exception *some need to be met* and out of that has come the procedure which in time crystallized into polity. In illustration we cite the trend denominationward, so very marked during the last one hundred years; unvaryingly it took its rise in the foreign missionary impulse. Local associations, together with their district and State conventions, might meet the demands for missionary work in their own or adjacent areas, whereas they felt powerless when they contemplated work in foreign lands. Such ventures implied a world-wide task of evangelization of such proportions as to demand a union of all the forces. The influence of William Carey called into being, in 1792, the English Baptist Missionary Society; which led on to the Baptist Union in 1832. The landing of Adoniram and Ann Hasseltine Judson in Burma, in 1813, created the General Convention of the Baptist Denomination in the United States for Foreign Missions, in the following year; a movement which has culminated in both the Southern and American Conventions. Only slightly later Canadian Baptists began to respond to the same missionary call. In 1846 the Baptist Convention of the Maritime Provinces united the two missionary societies located in Nova Scotia and New Brunswick. In 1888 an act of Parliament chartered the Ontario and Quebec Baptist Convention. The Baptist Union of Western Canada was formed in 1909. These three established conventions entered into close cooperation in 1944, by forming the Baptist Federation of Canada.

The significance of the missionary movement for Baptists themselves is nowhere better displayed than in the vast extensions of their polity. They were like mariners, swept to sea by a powerful outward-flowing tide, who had to meet new and critical situations by new seamanship. Baptists were embarked upon a world-wide enterprise which called to ways uncharted and unknown; their emerging polity is revealed in the " log " of their adventurous undertakings and achievements during the brief fourteen decades of their missionary history. The student thereof is impressed by initiative and daring, sacrifice and devotion, which bespeak a fulness of life seldom created save by the power of the pioneering urge. If Baptists have made missionary history, it is equally certain that the missionary movement has gone far toward making Baptists what they are, and Baptist polity what it is.

## Topics for Group Discussion

1. Resolved, that these more inclusive Conventions are inimical to the fullest development of the individual Christian.

2. Does the sense of responsibility for world-wide missionary work make centralization of promotional authority mandatory, or merely desirable?

3. Make a comparative study of the polity of the American and Southern Conventions, discovering in each items of superior merit.

4. Does the State convention make the Association a nearly useless bit of polity, or does it make it more essential?

5. Had we of this group been members of the Triennial Convention of 1844, would we have been among those endorsing a divisive policy?

6. Are Baptists of today in need of some new, challenging enterprise comparable to the foreign missionary call of one hundred, forty years ago? If so, would a crusade to establish peace, or to make the economic order a vehicle of righteousness, or the launching of a movement for ever widening interdenominational cooperation meet that need?

## Books Worth Consulting

Handy, Robert T., *We Witness Together*. The Friendship Press, New York, 1956.

Minutes and Year Books of the American Baptist Convention, Northern Baptist Convention, and various state conventions.

Newman, Albert H., *A History of the Baptist Churches in the United States*. The American Baptist Publication Society, Philadelphia, 1898.

Torbet, Robert G., *A History of the Baptists*. The Judson Press, Philadelphia, 1950; revised 1955.

### PRACTICAL SUGGESTIONS

Lead the group in preparing a graph that will set out in bold relief the organizational structure, including the local churches at one extreme and national conventions at the other. Create the spirit of friendly rivalry among the pupils as to who shall present the chart that is at once the neatest and the most comprehensive. The one adjudged the best may be displayed on the church bulletin-board or reproduced in the church calendar, as a means of instructing all the people.

## XI

# MORE INCLUSIVE GROUPINGS

### THE GENERAL CONVENTION OF BAPTISTS OF NORTH AMERICA

The dissolution, in 1844, of the Triennial Convention brought genuine pain and regret to the noblest spirits among Baptists both North and South. Though the conflicting tides of proslavery and antislavery feeling ran with violence, the leaders were not unmindful that little less than calamity had come to Kingdom interests as represented by Baptists. To suffer a division of forces while in the midst of great endeavor is serious beyond computation. The marvel is that the foreign missionary cause was not actually offered up as a sacrifice on the altar of sectional strife. That it was not is due to the genuine interest in that cause and the commendable restraint manifest in the severing of fraternal bonds.

But the Civil War is over. The third and fourth generations, since that regrettable conflict, are now coming into places of leadership within the denomination, and they are little concerned with the perpetuation of old animosities. Consequently, the feeling of Christian good-will yearly broadens and the conviction deepens that the rift of yesterday should be healed in this greater today. Each Convention has been, for many years, sending fraternal delegates to the other, and at times there have been other evidences of cooperation. It would seem, looking toward a reunion of the two great bodies, that there is no insuperable obstacle to that consummation.

# Polity and Practice in Baptist Churches

Nevertheless, there is found little sentiment for an organic union of the two divisions. In a hundred and thirteen years of independent life each has laid down its own polity and built thereon a great organization. Each has woven a complex fabric of good works, built a system of philanthropic and educational institutions after an elaborate pattern, developed world-wide missionary organizations, and on behalf of all these holds vast properties and endowments. With their thousands of churches they have been forged into denominational unities with characteristic and commendable loyalties.

It is thus evident how great would be the difficulties, practical and legal, that consolidation would face. Then, too, the results are visioned to be of doubtful value. The united whole might be unwieldy, and less effective and efficient than the parts now are. For example, two separate families in an area, working together as good neighbors, yet maintaining their own particular identities, mean more to the welfare of the community than would be the case should they attempt actual fusion. By the same token the existence of two great conventions, each leading its hosts in friendly rivalry (we stress *friendly* rivalry) as they promote Kingdom undertakings, are more potent than the one combined unit would be.

Nonetheless, there is an urgent need for more cooperation. Until the Communist regime disrupted our work in China, the two were cooperating in the University of Shanghai. They maintain the Joint Committee on Public Affairs. These are but meager beginnings in that cooperation which points the direction in which men of vision hope the two great bodies will march. It will be interesting to watch the growth of interdenominational polity as cooperation proceeds.

## More Inclusive Groupings

As early as 1905 the growing desire for strengthening the fraternal bonds between Northern and Southern Baptists issued in the launching of the General Convention of Baptists of North America, designed to " include the continent of North America and its islands." A declaration of objectives follows:

> The objects of this Convention shall be to promote closer fellowship among American Baptists, their increased efficiency and spirituality and the evangelistic spirit in our churches; to consider subjects having a bearing upon the missionary, educational, and philanthropic enterprises of the denomination and upon the moral and spiritual welfare of society.

According to which it is clear that the purpose was fraternal and educative; a most laudable move, it would be generally agreed.

This Convention was called into being in St. Louis, Missouri, at the conclusion of simultaneous meetings of Northern and Southern groups in Kansas City and St. Louis, respectively. The Hon. E. W. Stevens, president of the Southern Convention, was chosen president. Having completed the organization, it was agreed to arrange the first continent-wide convocation for the following year, 1906; and thereafter every third year.

In the meantime the city of Jamestown, Virginia, founded in 1607, was vigorously appealing to the nation on behalf of the Jamestown Exposition, in honor of its three-hundredth anniversary. It was decided therefore to call the first meeting of the General Convention in this historic city of the Southland, for 1907, at a date immediately following the adjournment of the May meetings, of Northern Baptists, that year scheduled for Washington. But something happened at these same May meetings;

the Northern Baptist Convention was organized over the protest of the chief Northern promoters of the General Convention, who apparently were interested in the latter largely as a ruse by means of which to postpone, if not actually defeat, the persistent movement for a Northern Baptist Convention.

At least those close to the General Convention so interpreted following events. The scheduled meetings for Jamestown were held, but the attendance was very small from both sections of the country. Most marked was the absence of the Northern leaders who had been the chief promoters of the " Convention to promote closer fellowship among American Baptists." The practical failure of this meeting was sufficient to kill the General Convention. There has been no serious attempt to resuscitate it. Decently interred, its gravestone might read: "A noble and needed creation. Died in infancy. Sacrificed on the altar of ecclesiastical politics. May the day of resurrection come." As a matter of interest we give excerpts from the Constitution:

### ARTICLE I

#### NAME AND TERRITORY

The objects of this Convention shall be to promote closer fellow-of Baptists of North America. It shall include the continent of North America and its islands.

### ARTICLE II

#### OBJECTS

The objects of this Convention shall be to promote closer fellowship among American Baptists, their increased efficiency and spirituality and the evangelistic spirit in our churches; to consider subjects having a bearing upon the missionary, educational, and philanthropic enterprises of the denomination and upon the moral and spiritual welfare of society.

## ARTICLE III

### LIMITATIONS

This Convention shall exercise no authority other than that which the weight of its opinions may carry, nor shall it interfere with the churches or with the missionary or educational agencies of the denomination.

## ARTICLE IV

### MEMBERSHIP

This Convention shall be composed of representatives duly appointed as follows:

SECTION 1. Each church may appoint one representative, and one additional representative for every one hundred members or fraction thereof above the first one hundred.

SEC. 2. Each local or district Association may appoint two representatives, and one additional representative for every ten churches or fraction thereof above the first ten.

SEC. 3. Each territorial, provincial, and State Convention (or general Association) may appoint ten representatives, and one additional representative for every ten thousand members above the first fifty thousand.

## BY-LAWS

The Convention shall meet in 1906, and thereafter every three years; the exact time and place to be determined by the Executive Committee. Special meetings of the Convention may be called upon petition of two hundred members of Baptist churches, whose residences shall be in at least ten States or Provinces, and upon approval of the petition by the majority of the Executive Committee.

## THE BAPTIST WORLD ALLIANCE

Baptists number about twenty millions, scattered throughout many nations. Being democratic in polity and life, the thousands of churches have only spiritual unity. The absence of a deeper sense of world-wide fraternity and denominational solidarity is cause for regret. How great is this lack and how great a need it bespeaks is seen when one views the Baptists in contrast with such other Protestant groups as the Lutherans and Episcopalians. A desire to develop the sense of a world-wide oneness was long felt among Baptist leaders. Accordingly, the same year, 1905, that witnessed the birth of the General Convention of Baptists of North America saw also the convening in London of the Baptist World Congress. It was a great day for Baptists; they assembled from nations that circle the globe; and from July 11 to 19 they fellowshiped together after a fashion known only to those closely akin in soul-gripping concerns. The Congress, presided over by the venerable Alexander McLaren, was such a notable success that it culminated in the launching of The Baptist World Alliance, a permanent organization. It intended to meet every five years, a schedule that has been fairly well maintained, save for World War interferences. The Preamble to the Constitution of the Alliance is worthy of reprint and study:

The Baptist World Alliance, extending over every part of the world, exists in order more fully to show the essential oneness of Baptist people in the Lord Jesus Christ, to impart inspiration to the brotherhood, and to promote the spirit of fellowship, service and co-operation among its members; but this Alliance may in no way interfere with the independence of the churches or assume the administrative functions of existing organizations.

First of all this preamble voices the need for greater oneness; an essential oneness, we note, of Baptist people in the Lord Jesus Christ, to impart inspiration to the brotherhood, and to promote the spirit of fellowship, service, and cooperation among its members. And in order that churches and other organizations may be assured that no overhead control of their affairs is in any wise contemplated, this preamble makes a specific promise of noninterference. Membership in the Alliance may be held by any general Union, Convention, or Association of Baptist Churches, each of which may appoint messengers to the General Meeting on a basis to be determined by the Executive Committee. So in this most distant and all-inclusive outreach of Baptist polity there is manifest the same unabridged democracy that constitutes the genius of the local church.

Those accustomed to highly centralized, ecclesiastical unities may think this Baptist unity the merest shadow of reality. We do not share their conviction. Here is a democratic unity, a unity of mind and spirit, freely begotten, which is the only vital and living unity. Such may have, and does have, promotional inefficiency, but it possesses a life-building effectiveness unknown, we fear, to mere organizational unity. These principles may be seen in the following excerpts from the Constitution as amended at the Ninth World Congress, London, 1955.

### II. Nature and Functions

Serving as the nerve center and corporate will of Baptists throughout the world the Alliance shall:

(1) Have as one of its primary purposes the safeguarding and maintenance of full religious liberty everywhere, not only for our own constituent churches, but also for all other religious faiths.

(2) Serve as an agency for propagating Baptist principles and tenets of faith, objectives and distinctive principles throughout the world.

(3) Serve as an agency to make surveys throughout the world with a view to furnishing facts to the various Baptist groups and counselling with them in establishing work in new fields when such service is requested.

(4) Serve as a world-wide agency in making such use of the radio and press as may be practicable in preaching the Gospel, propagating Baptist principles, and promoting common tasks of Baptists throughout the world.

(5) Arrange and conduct preaching missions throughout the world.

(6) Co-operate with Baptist groups in instituting and administering relief funds as occasion may require.

(7) Gather news by means of correspondents in the various Baptist groups, and disseminate it by use of bulletins, Baptist and

other papers, and radio; and, when feasible, by a Baptist world publication.

In ministering in any one or all of these fields of service, the Baptist World Alliance shall limit its activities strictly within its annual budget.

## III. *Membership*

Any general Union, Convention, or Association of Baptist churches, or general Foreign Baptist Missionary Society, or Conference of Baptist churches on a mission field, which is not already an integral part of a Convention, shall be eligible for membership in the Alliance subject to the approval of the Executive Committee.

## V. *Executive Committee*

The Executive Committee shall consist of the Officers of the Alliance, Past Presidents, Past General Secretaries, and thirty-nine other members who shall be elected at the General Meeting of the Alliance, and shall enter on office at the close of such meeting. These thirty-nine shall represent all six continents as provided in the By-laws, due consideration being given to the geographical distribution of Vice-Presidents and Treasurers. The Executive Committee shall also have power to co-opt not more than nine additional members. The Women's Department and the Youth Department shall each nominate two members to the Executive.

## VI. *Functions of the Executive Committee*

It shall be the function of the Executive Committee:

(1) To transact the business of the Alliance between General Meetings, and to supervise the administration of any undertaking projected by the Alliance.

(2) To appoint an Administrative Sub-Committee as indicated in VII below, and to appoint such standing or special committees as it may deem necessary, and to determine their duties.

(3) To arrange local, regional, continental or other conferences as may be considered desirable.

(4) To fill vacancies in the offices and in the committees of the Alliance.

(5) To fix the time and place of the General Meeting of the Alliance, unless these have been determined by the Alliance in General Meeting, and to make all necessary arrangements therefor, including the preparation of the program.

(6) To nominate for appointment by the Alliance in General Meeting, a Nominating Committee, a Business Committee, a Resolutions Committee, and other committees to serve during the sessions of the General Meeting.

## VII. *Administrative Sub-Committee*

The Executive Committee shall appoint from its members an Administrative Sub-Committee of seven including at least one woman. The members of this committee shall reside within reasonable distance of the headquarters city of the Alliance, and serve as an Advisory Committee to the General Secretary, and shall have power to act for the Executive Committee *ad interim* with the understanding that all its actions shall be reported promptly to the members of the Executive Committee.

The President of the Alliance, the General Secretary, the Western Hemisphere Treasurer, and such ex-Presidents and Vice-Presidents as live within reasonable distance from the headquarters of the Alliance shall be *ex-officio* members of the Administrative Sub-Committee.

The Administrative Sub-Committee, in co-operation with the General Secretary and Treasurers, shall be charged with the responsibility of soliciting funds for the support of the Alliance. The sources of income shall be an appropriation by each constituent Convention, Union, or Association within the Alliance, free-will offerings by local churches on Baptist World Alliance Sunday, and voluntary gifts.

The Administrative Sub-Committee, with the General Secretary and Treasurers, shall be charged with the responsibility of submitting each year a proposed budget to the Executive Committee, which committee shall have full authority to act on the budget.

### VIII. Meetings

The Alliance shall assemble in General Meeting ordinarily not less than once in five years.

### IX. Representation in General Meeting

Each body represented in the Alliance may appoint messengers to the General Meeting on a basis to be determined by the Executive Committee.

### X. Amendments

No change shall be made in this Constitution except by a two-thirds majority of those present and voting at a General Meeting after at least two days' notice of the proposed action.

Perhaps one may scarcely overestimate the significance and achievements of the Baptist World Alliance. The programs of the various meetings have been conceived to facilitate an exchange of views on many matters and as a means of creating inspiration for a world-wide witness. But we believe they have succeeded far beyond that designed measure.

## Polity and Practice in Baptist Churches

The first great ministry of the Alliance is the growing of a Baptist consciousness around the world. Baptists of many nations are rapidly coming to feel a fine sense of solidarity, a oneness in the spirit of Christ, and are bearing their witness with new strength and assurance. This accomplishment is well not only for the Baptist people, but for the ongoing of the kingdom of God; surely so if, as we believe, Baptists have a vital message to be delivered.

Moreover the Alliance has been used by God to bring new assurance and courage to smaller and scattered groups of Baptists. These are often peoples who labor in vineyards that are stubborn and little rewarding yet of untold import in the divine economy of Kingdom progress. To have brought new heart to such as these has in itself justified the Alliance.

Not only so, beyond this the stronger Baptist constituencies have been led to discover their brethren who compose smaller and weaker groups and have been moved to bring aid both in terms of counsel and money. This is particularly true as regards the deep concern of English and American Baptists for those who bear the Baptist witness in the many nations of the Continent. These countries are not considered mission fields, but are viewed rather as areas wherein the Protestant Reformation should be revived and encouraged, to complete the work long ago begun.

Beyond these considerations the Alliance has achieved no inconsiderable beginning toward making the Christian world conscious that there is a people called Baptists, that they number many millions, that they have a notable record of commendable accomplishment, and that they conceive themselves sent of God to bear a very certain and positive witness for Christ among the nations. In so far as this objective has been attained it can be thought second only in importance to the service of the Alliance to the Baptists themselves. The Alliance, meeting in Stockholm, July, 1923, adopted a Message and sent it to the world as the embodiment of that gospel which Baptists proclaim.

### A MESSAGE OF THE BAPTIST WORLD ALLIANCE TO THE BAPTIST BROTHERHOOD, TO OTHER CHRISTIAN BRETHREN, AND TO THE WORLD

*The Third Baptist World Congress, meeting in Stockholm, Sweden, July, 1923, and representing with few exceptions the Baptists of every country in the world, a constituency numbering ten millions of baptized members, and many millions of adherents, in view of world conditions, and resolutely facing the problems of the future, makes this statement of Baptist principles and purposes to the Christians and peoples of the world.*

We are, first and always, Christians, acknowledging in its deepest and broadest sense the Lordship of Jesus Christ, and devoted to Him as the Son of God and Saviour of the world. We rejoice that the spiritual unity of all believers is a blessed reality, not dependent upon organization or ceremonies. We pray that by increasing obedience to Christ's will, this unity may be deepened and strengthened among Christians of every name.

#### THE LORDSHIP OF JESUS CHRIST

There are various ways of stating the fundamental Baptist principle. If we indicate the source of our knowledge, we say the scriptures of the Old and New Testaments are divinely inspired, and are our sufficient, certain, and authoritative guide in all matters of faith and practice. As to the nature of the Christian religion, we affirm that it is personal and spiritual. We believe in the direct relation of each individual to God, and the right of everyone to choose for himself in all matters of faith. A Christian's religion begins in the soul when personal faith is exercised in Jesus Christ, the divine Redeemer and Lord. As the Revealer of God to men and the Mediator of salvation, Jesus Christ is central for Christian faith. His will is the supreme law for the Christian. He is Lord of the conscience of the individual and of the Church. Hence, the Lordship of Jesus Christ is a cardinal teaching of Baptists. It excludes all merely human authorities in religion.

### The Nature of Baptist Unity

We desire to impress upon our Baptist brethren in every part of the world the importance of Baptist unity at the present time. Accepting the voluntary principle in religion and regarding the nature of Christianity as a spiritual relation between man and God, we inevitably take the same attitude on questions of faith and conduct as they arise within the churches. We hold fast to the freedom with which Christ has set us free, and this principle implies that we must be willing to love and to work with those who, agreeing with us on the main things and in loyalty to our distinctive Baptist principles, have their own personal convictions upon non-essentials. All Baptist organizations are formed on the voluntary principle. None of these possesses authority over any other. All enjoy equal rights and autonomy within the limits of their own purposes.

### Christian Unity

Baptists have ever held all who have communion with God in our Lord Jesus Christ as our Christian brethren in the work of the Lord, and heirs with us of eternal life. We love their fellowship, and maintain that the spiritual union does not depend upon organization, forms, or ritual. It is deeper, higher, broader, and more stable than any or all externals. All who truly are joined to Christ are our brethren in the common salvation, whether they be in the Catholic communion, or in a Protestant communion, or in any other communion, or in no communion. Baptists, with all evangelical Christians, rejoice in the common basic beliefs; the incarnation of the Son of God, His sinless life, His supernatural works, His Deity, His vicarious atonement and resurrection from the dead, His present reign and His coming kingdom, with its eternal awards to the righteous and unrighteous.

To Baptists it is entirely clear that the direct relation of the soul to God, or the universal priesthood of believers, is the basis of the New Testament teaching as to the church and the ministry. Christian unity, therefore, as Baptists understand the New Testament, is a result of the operation of the Holy Spirit arising from a common faith in Christ, enlightened by a common understanding of His teachings, inspired by a common vision of the ends of the Kingdom of God, and issuing in a free and voluntary cooperation in the execution of the will of Christ. Christian unity is thus a flexible principle, adapting itself to every situation. It admits cooperation so far as there is agreement, and abstains from all coercion.

The implications of the voluntary principle based upon the universal priesthood of believers in their bearing upon Christian unity are clear. Baptists cannot consent to any form of union which impairs the rights of the individual believer. We cannot unite with others in any centralized ecclesiastical organization wielding power over the individual conscience. We cannot accept the sacerdotal conception of the ministry which involves the priesthood of a class with special powers for transmitting grace. We cannot accept the conception of ordination made valid through a historic succession in the ministry. As Baptists understand the New Testament, all believers being priests unto God, ministers can possess no further sacerdotal powers. They are called to special tasks of preaching and teaching and administration. They remain the spiritual equals of other believers in the church. Again, the principle of the universal priesthood of believers involves the direct authority of Jesus Christ, our Great High Priest. Christian unity, therefore, can only come through obedience to the will of Christ as revealed in the New Testament, which Baptists must ever take as their sole, sufficient, certain, and authoritative guide.

### The Baptist Faith and Mission

As Baptists view it, the Christian religion finds its central truth in the incarnation of God in Jesus Christ, whose sinless life and heavenly wisdom, whose Deity, atoning death, resurrection from the dead, and whose second coming and lordship in the Kingdom of God constitute and qualify him for his work as its Founder and Mediator. God calls all men to salvation through him, in whom they are freely justified by grace through faith, and regenerated by the operation of the Holy Spirit. Regeneration, or the new birth, is a necessary condition of church-membership, since in this way alone can the churches be kept spiritual and responsive to the will of Christ. Church-membership of believers only is a fundamental Baptist principle. Each church, as made up of the regenerate, is competent to conduct its own affairs. It is, therefore, by its nature and constitution, a spiritual democracy, free and self-governing, and answering to Christ alone as its ultimate authority.

The New Testament recognizes nothing as baptism but the immersion in water of the believer upon profession of faith. In the Lord's Supper it recognizes no sacerdotal authority in those who administer it, and no sacramental quality in the bread and wine, by virtue of which it conveys grace through any change in the elements.

In the matter of the polity, the officers, and the ordinances of a church, Baptists seek to preserve the spirituality and simplicity of the New Testament, and at the same time the proper proportion of emphasis. A group of great spiritual principles underlies their conception of a church at all points. As a self-governing spiritual democracy, a church recognizes the spiritual competency and freedom of the individual members. Since it requires a personal profession of faith as a condition of baptism, it eliminates the proxy element in faith and respects the rights of personality. Hence, infant baptism is utterly irreconcilable with the ideal of a spiritual Christianity. Voluntary and not compulsory baptism is a vital spiritual principle of the New Testament.

The officers of a church are teachers and leaders, not ecclesiastical authorities. Thus at all points a church of Christ is the outward expression of great spiritual principles; the supreme value of personality, the inalienable rights of free choice and of direct access to God, the equality of all believers, and their common spiritual priesthood. No charge, therefore, can be more groundless than that Baptists are ceremonialists or sacramentalists. They are the exact opposite of these things.

In harmony with the above principles, Baptists conceive their mission to the world to be moral and spiritual. Primarily, their duty is to make known the will of Christ and secure the willing submission of men to him, as set forth in the gospel of the grace of God. Evangelization and missions thus become prime factors in the programme of Baptists. The command of Christ to preach the gospel to every creature is of permanent binding force. The necessity for education, philanthropy, and civic and social righteousness in manifold forms arises inevitably out of evangelizing and missionary activity.

### RELIGIOUS LIBERTY AND ITS APPLICATIONS

Baptists from the beginning of their history have been the ardent champions of religious liberty. They have often been persecuted, but they could never persecute others save in defiance of their own principles. Religious liberty is an inherent and inalienable human right. It arises out of the direct relation of the soul to God. Man is constituted in God's image. He is a free personality. Moral responsibility is based upon this freedom. This is a fundamental axiom of ethics as well as of religion.

Religious liberty, in its broadest significance, implies the following elements: First, no human authority of any kind, in society at large, in church or state, has any right to repress or hinder or thwart any man or group of men in the exercise of religious belief or worship. Second, the right of every man and group of men to complete freedom in the search for, the worship of, and obedience to God. Third, freedom to teach and preach those beliefs and truths which men may hold as committed to them from God to be made known to others.

Religious liberty is inconsistent with any union of church and state, because the church rests upon the spiritual principle of free choice, while the state rests upon law with an ultimate appeal to physical force. It is inconsistent with special favour by the state towards one or more religious groups and toleration towards others, because equality of privilege is a fundamental and inalienable religious right of all men. It is inconsistent with priestly and episcopal authority and with infant baptism, because free choice and voluntary obedience to Christ are essential to the Christian religion.

Thus Baptists stand for the rights of the individual versus the close ecclesiastical corporation, the direct relation of the soul to God versus the indirect, free grace versus sacramental grace, believer's baptism versus infant baptism, personal versus proxy faith, the priesthood of all believers versus the priesthood of a class, democracy in the church versus autocracy or oligarchy or other forms of human authority. Religious liberty is not license. It gives no right to the indulgence of lust or sin in any form. It confers no exemption from the authority of the state in its own sphere. It implies and requires loyalty to Christ on the part of every Christian. For non-Christians it implies responsibility to God alone for religious beliefs, and freedom from all coercion in matters of religious opinion. Baptists have ever insisted upon religious freedom for unbelievers and atheists, as well as Christians. However deplorable their unbelief, they are responsible not to human authorities but to God.

### RELIGION AND ETHICS

Our religion is not only for the salvation of the individual, it is also ethical and social. The new life in Christ creates a new moral character and a new sense of social responsibility. The Christian ideal is God's Kingdom. He is to reign in all realms of life. His will is to rule in the family, in the church, in industry, in society, in the arts, in the state, and in international relations.

### FAMILY LIFE

Family life of high quality is fundamental to all human progress. Here especially should personality, its needs, its discipline and development, control. Here Christ's law of mutual love and service should rule. Children are free personalities to be reared in the nurture and admonition of the Lord. The will is not to be broken, but disciplined and trained. The home should be a living fountain of religious life, where prayer and study of the Scriptures should not be shifted to the school or to any other agency. Divorce on unscriptural grounds is one of the greatest evils of the day in many parts of the world. The duty of all Christians everywhere is to resist this evil. Christ's teaching on the subject should be respected, and every proper means employed to resist and correct the tendency to divorce. The sacredness of the marriage vow, and the purity of home life should be safeguarded in all possible ways.

### CHRISTIANITY AND SOCIAL QUESTIONS

There is widely apparent in the churches today the growth of a new conscience in relation to social problems and a new quest for the will of God in modern society. We are realizing afresh that the purpose of Christianity is the purification of the entire life of humanity, its end a community truly and completely Christian. The noble and self-sacrificing work of caring for the social wreckage of our time, the poverty-stricken and the outcast, must not cease. But our duty does not end there. Not simply by doing an honest day's work, or by cultivating relations of brotherhood with one's fellow-workers, important as these are, can the Christian obligation be fully met. We must strive also to the end that the organization of society itself shall accord with Christ's will, as well as that one's calling within society shall be conformable thereto.

Baptists gladly recognize the Christian duty of applying the teaching and spirit of our Lord to social, industrial, and family relations. While not committed to any of the varied and conflicting theories of economics, we affirm the Christian conception of industrial relations to be cooperation rather than competition. Life is a stewardship held for the enrichment of all, and not simply for personal gain.

We stand for world peace through international courts of justice, industrial peace through obedience to the rule of Christ, "Do unto others as ye would they should do unto you," domestic peace by acceptance of the sanctity of the marriage bond and the parental responsibility to train children in the nurture and love of the Lord.

### CHRISTIAN STEWARDSHIP

Christian Stewardship rests upon the foundation of God's ownership of ourselves and our possessions. "Ye are not your own. Ye have been bought with a price," is the divine declaration. All wealth is to be held in trust as God's gift. It is to be used as He commands. The right of private ownership of property by the Christian does not mean the right to do as he wills with his own, but rather as God wills. The mere accumulation of wealth is not the aim of the Christian business man, but rather the use of wealth in the service of God and men. Under the old dispensation the Jews gave at least one-tenth of their income to the service of God. Christians are not under law but under the gospel. But surely their obligation requires giving upon a scale equal to that of Jews. One tenth, however, does not exhaust the Christian's obligation. All that he has belongs to God, and his giving should be in proportion to the needs and requirements of the Lord's work and his own ability, whether it be one-tenth or nine-tenths or even more of his income.

## THE SABBATH

We recognize and reaffirm with vigor the sanctity of the Sabbath; all work, except works of necessity and mercy, should be avoided on the Sabbath day. God has appointed one day in seven as a day of rest and worship, and it should be observed by all men in accordance with the divine command. We condemn as unchristian the commercialization of the Sabbath day in the interest of business or amusement of any kind. As a civil institution, one day in seven, observed as a day of rest, has proved to be in the highest degree promotive of human welfare. The religious observance of the Sabbath as a day of worship is a matter for free and voluntary action. Laws to compel such observance are opposed to religious liberty. But laws to protect the Sabbath as a civil institution are right and should be enforced.

## TEMPERANCE

We record our conviction that the modern movement to curb traffic in strong drink for beverage purposes is of God. We believe that governments should recognize the movement and that instead of deriving support from it through taxation, should abolish this traffic.

## BAPTISTS AND LOYALTY TO STATE

Baptists have always been a loyal and patriotic people. This attitude arises out of their fundamental principles. It is a necessary result of their submission to the will of God as revealed in Jesus Christ. It is seen clearly in the light of their view of the State and of the Church. Baptists believe that the State is ordained of God. It is established to restrain and punish the evildoer and for the protection of human rights. It is, therefore, essential to human welfare. It is not to be used in the interest of any group or class, but to promote the common good. Its duty is to safeguard the personal, economic, civic and religious rights of all.

It thus appears that the work of the church and the work of

the State lie in different spheres. In the one case it is a spiritual, in the other a political task. There is no antagonism, and there should be no conflict. Each should freely pursue its own tasks in its own department of life by its own means and methods. Neither should seek to thwart or hinder the other. The members of the churches should obey the laws of the State as loyal citizens or subjects. The State should protect the rights of all men of various religious beliefs. The supreme loyalty of all men is to God. Disobedience to the State, therefore, is never justified except when the State usurps the place of God in trying to compel the conscience in religious matters, or when it becomes a transgressor of the law of God in requiring what is in violation of Divine commands.

## INTERNATIONAL RELATIONS

Nations are morally bound to each other. The State, like the individual, must be regarded as a member of a larger community in which other members possess rights similar to its own. This implies that in an orderly world there can be no real conflict of interests between various governments. Secret, selfish diplomacy and intrigue are crying sins before God. National selfishness is a terrible evil.

We record our profound conviction against war. It is destructive of all economic, moral and spiritual values. A war of aggression is a direct contradiction of every principle of the Gospel of Christ. It violates the ideals of peace and brotherhood and is inconsistent with the law of love. It alienates nations which Christ seeks to unify in bonds of friendship. It enthrones hate and dries up the fountains of sympathy. It sets power above right. It creates burdensome debts. It is prodigal in its waste of life.

The true remedy for war is the Gospel of Christ. The new birth by God's Spirit creates divine love within the soul of the individual. The law of God is thus written upon the heart. The greatest need of the world is acceptance of the Lordship of Christ, by men everywhere, and practical application of His law of love.

We favor cooperation among the nations of the world to promote peace. No nation can live an isolated life. To attempt to do so inevitably gives rise to complicated problems and leads to conflict in many forms. The good of all is the good of each, and the good of each is the good of all. Christ's law of service is the key to all human progress. Nations as well as individuals are bound by that law. By obedience to it shall we hasten the complete realization of God's will among men and the fulfilment of the ideals of the great prayer which the Master taught us to pray: "Thy Kingdom come. Thy will be done on earth as in heaven."

We believe that the world has come to a parting of the ways. It is another coming of the Son of Man. It is another Day of the Lord. The question is whether the world will pass along the way of order and peace and goodness and faith, or whether it will go down into scepticism and materialism. We believe that the simple message of the Baptists with its union of gospel and ethics, of faith and practice, with its note of freedom, democracy, spirituality, will find an answering chord in this new world.

## Topics for Group Discussion

1. Discuss the proposition that the time has come for a close affiliation, if not actual union, of Northern and Southern Baptist Conventions.

2. *Resolved,* That in the work of education on the foreign mission fields not only should Baptists of the North and South cooperate, but they should seek wherever possible cooperation with other Protestant groups.

3. Catalog all the good reasons you can to justify The Baptist World Alliance.

## Books and Periodicals Worth Consulting

Baillie, Donald M. and Marsh, John, eds. *Intercommunion.* Harper and Brothers, New York, 1952.

Baptist Periodicals.

Baptist World Congress, 1905, London. Official proceedings.

Baptist World Alliance, 1923, Stockholm. Official proceedings.

Baptist World Alliance, 1928, Toronto. Record of proceedings.

Baptist World Alliance, 1934, Berlin. Record of proceedings.

Baptist World Alliance, 1939, Atlanta. Record of proceedings.

Baptist World Alliance, 1947, Copenhagen. Record of proceedings.

Baptist World Alliance, 1950, Cleveland. Record of proceedings.

Baptist World Alliance, 1955, London. Record of proceedings.

### PRACTICAL SUGGESTIONS

1. Study, section by section, the "Message" of the Alliance sent out from Stockholm, in order that your group may come to sense the scope and vitality of the gospel that Baptists preach.

2. As a group project, inspire the group to make Baptist World Alliance scrapbooks. Such should include snapshots of the most recent meeting of the Alliance, photographs of officers and other notable participants, together with a thumbnail biography of each, and his place among Baptists. Make a record of outstanding addresses given, either in digest or outline form; etc. The idea will grow as the books progress and interest quickens.

3. Note the date and place of the next meeting of the Alliance, and plan to aid one or more members of the group to attend. Whether or not this be achieved, let the progress of the meetings be followed by means of the daily and religious journals—thus adding a current chapter to scrap-books.

# XII

## COOPERATIVE UNITY, FEDERATION, ORGANIC UNION

Baptists were born of conviction—and tribulation. Of all the non-conformists they were among the most determined, and hence suffered the greater persecution. They were victimized, not only by the established order, but by other non-conformists as well. They were esteemed of all heretics the worst! Naturally, therefore, when any semblance of liberty of conscience or freedom in religion did come to them, they hedged it about with most jealous care. Not only so, they drew to themselves and began to build their own tower and fortress.

In consequence Baptists became a rather exclusive people; fearful of association with others, thinking that thereby they might run the risk of losing their jewels of liberty and independency. This temper is seen even in the relation of church to church. The close communion practice is a plant indigenous to that soil—justified, of course, by the Scriptures! And how cautiously the churches at first approached each other in the Associations! No one may peruse the early documents without discovering restraint and hesitancy. The first Associations were evidently viewed as a venture. Only after much experiment does there arise anything detectable as genuine fellowship. An inborn fear driving toward seclusion was long at war with the necessity of fraternal connections for the sake of mutual counsel and strength. The Associations, State Conventions, and every other enlargement of cooperative polity, have uniformly been met by the same fear and hesitancy. Every step in that direction has been forced by the necessities of new needs.

Baptists are children of the past as well as of the present. No people, not even the Baptists, can escape the influence of their history. An unseen hand reaches out of the past to check and restrain. It is little wonder therefore that Baptists have developed not only solidarity but also—at times—clannishness. Their very past makes for exclusiveness, sectarianism. Few bodies of Christians have been slower than they to develop cooperative tendencies.

Perhaps this is unfortunate. The spirit of the age is making for closer coordination and larger cooperation in every field of human endeavor. Religious enterprise cannot escape its influence if it would. Churches, groups, denominations are drawing together on many fronts. In such a day Baptist exclusiveness may be interpreted as a virtue or a vice, depending upon one's point of view. One person may call it loyalty, another bigotry. But anyone who knows the history of this people sees the logic of their caution. Even so, the day for sectarianism is past. The forces that make for the coming of the kingdom of God must present an unbroken front to a stubborn world. Divisions constitute a published weakness, and the spirit of non-cooperation a thing intolerable. The closing of the ranks on the part of all those who constitute the marching hosts of the Lord is Kingdom strategy for our day. The command, " Fall into line! " is on the morning air; Baptists and all others must hear and obey.

" Fall into line! " what shall this mean for Baptists? That they, like others, hear the command is certain, but just how to execute it is the problem. Conformity, the child of command and coercion, is not of their genius. This is the vexatious question that today confronts Baptist statesmanship. Cooperate Baptists must, but the polity of Protestantism is divisive, not cooperative, and Baptist polity turns inward toward isolation. New lines of polity must be projected in the direction of widening cooperation with all the forces of the kingdom of Christ.

From the independency of the local church as an ideal to interdenominational cooperation as a practical policy is, for Baptists, a distance of many long leagues. No body save the Roman Catholics has a greater mileage to cover before they strike hands with other Christians in the common task of enlarging the borders of the kingdom of God. Yet to be deterred by the size of the problem is to be unworthy of the past. The fathers made a way by force through their difficulties and thereby wrought a polity—that is, a way of doing things—consistent at once with soul competency and the work that must be done. Their hands were not bound; neither are the hands of their progeny, the Baptists of today.

Never were the lines more closely drawn between the church and the world than today. The forces of the latter show an appalling solidarity as they oppose themselves to those who make for righteousness in the earth. Compelled thereby, the churches and the denominations, now beginning to close their ranks, are developing a new polity in three areas. These we may designate as the area of cooperative unity, the area of federation, and the area of organic union. Let us see what Baptists are doing in these matters.

Cooperative unity is the area adjacent to every church, whether in city, village, or open country. The city church, of all denominations, is literally surrounded by other churches with which it may cooperate, yes, ought to co-operate, in the discharge of not a few common tasks. The village church invariably has neighboring churches—alas! often they are competing churches—with which there is opportunity of cooperation for the community good; and the church in the open country is seldom removed too far from other churches for united effort on behalf of neighborhood welfare and good-will. And what is true of churches is doubly true of the denominations; they are ever not only adjacent but overlapping. They often jostle each other for place while there is ample opportunity and pressing need for cooperation. Whether in country, village, or city the denominations and all their churches should be presenting a solid front in terms of cooperation.

We say that cooperative unity is adjacent, by which we mean that in local areas the opportunity for unity of action is nearest to hand. In this area the Baptist churches are today not lagging behind others. The increasing frequency with which the united churches of a given area are developing a program of action is commendable. They are thus marching forth to destroy the strongholds of evil and to build instead the towers of righteousness. They are sitting in council concerning various programs for the general good; a significant gain when a given area is viewed as something to be developed into a community rather than something to be exploited for divisive interests. All this is praiseworthy and hopeful. And as the experimentation progresses—for experimentation it is—the polity of cooperation is being grown. There are still sections (we speak of the United States) where Baptists maintain their historic exclusiveness and block united undertakings. Such an attitude is increasingly difficult to condone, whether in Baptists or in others.

It should be noted here that those communities whose churches are working shoulder to shoulder in constructive effort are loudest in their praise of the widening cooperation. Some such movements have failed, it is regrettable to record, because the object was wholly to attack and destroy " works of evil." As is so often true, the frontal attack has proved foolhardy and in truth undoing. Wiser is discovered to be that procedure which aims to uproot by indirection, that is by planting the good that it may grow up and choke the evil. All cooperative efforts thrive best as they build up the structure of good in the area over which they operate, leaving to rare occasions of extreme provocation the work of denunciation and demolition. Better let sleeping dogs lie, meanwhile administering the anæsthetic of constructive good works—so experience counsels.

The area of cooperative unity lies adjacent to denominations also. Their lines run out " through all the earth," as the Psalmist might say. Unfortunately these lines do not always merely run parallel; quite generally they constitute a fabric of crisscross pattern. Nevertheless they *are* adjacent. The tangled skein of interests does not change that fact. How to untangle the skein and weave a new fabric, after the pattern of cooperative effort, is the problem.

Each major denomination has manifested zeal in the planting of new churches, mostly by the agency of domestic missionary societies. By such they have pushed into remoter regions with the pioneer and followed along with those who were builders of new empires. Not infrequently the zeal of one denomination came into conflict with that of another, with the result that most communities are sinfully overchurched. The fruit of such a condition is not pleasant to contemplate. Its influence for ill has been greatest in rural and small-town areas. In these a competitive denominationalism has been divisive to community interests and paralyzing to wholesome religious life. Fulness of life cannot flourish in the atmosphere of petty sectarianism. Much as we might desire, we cannot venture to claim that Baptists have sinned less than others in these regards. In fact, their "zealousness" has been second to none; and sometimes its expression has been of little credit to them or the Master's cause.

The missionary agencies: State conventions and home mission societies, which have so splendidly wrought in carrying the gospel into distant parts—their very zeal has sometimes betrayed them. It is they who are today confronted by the appeal for cooperative unity. They are challenged thereby not only not to commit again the wrongs of yesterday, but to attempt their righting. The route to such a goal is that of cooperative action on the part of these same agencies, and cooperation across denominational lines. Not only that wrongs may be righted, but also that thousands of communities may be served the better, thanks to the disappearance of competition and its herd of attendant evils.

As yet there is no great response on the part of Baptists, or others, to this challenge of cooperative unity. Lines of polity have become rigid, and are sustained by the conservatism of the denominations. But here and there a leader lifts his voice against the waste of missionary funds in competitive effort, and with increasing frequency the churches are withholding moneys from such enterprises. These are signs which he who can read the skies of a new day may discern. Some tomorrow, at no great distance removed, will decree the end of all such business, in the interest of the unchurched.

Wherever this problem is being honestly faced by denominational boards and their executives there is heard the magic word, " comity." When comity becomes operative it puts an end to competition; it brings into conference responsible parties who seek means of avoiding or removing damaging competition. For instance, a certain community of fifteen hundred souls is now being served by five churches, whereas it would be far better served by two of these, at the most. The executives of the five denominations concerned sit in conference, and agree that three bodies should withdraw from the field; withdrawal by each of the three executives urging his constituency to disband and giving notice that denominational funds will no longer be forthcoming in support of their projects. Or if this be a new community, wherein churches are yet to be established, a similar conference would decide that only two denominations should enter the field, the others agreeing to keep out. The three thus relinquishing their free right to enter, or, as in the former case, withdrawing after once being established, these will be given priority in some other community where their situation is more favorable. By such a policy the various communities would be spared the evils of competing churches. In the end each denomination would be the better off.

Naturally, the practical difficulties of administration under such a policy are great; precisely proportionate to the violence and sinfulness of sectarian competition. Each denomination is perfectly willing to have the others withdraw, but when the tables turn, it is a different matter. Too many Baptists feel that way. Their feelings are tuned to the same pitch as are religious prejudices;

and so long as that is true, cooperative unity can make no headway.

Nevertheless, advances in cooperation are being made. Although there still are some who are heedless of the ultimate gains to be made, there are increasing numbers of denominations and congregations which happily work with fellow Christians in other communions. An early example was the cooperation in the Montana and Idaho Baptist State Conventions. Dr. W. A. Shanks, who was executive secretary of the former, wrote:

Since the Home Missions Council of Idaho made a survey of the State . . . and provided for the allocation of various fields, there has been a wonderful spirit of cooperation on the part of the Protestant denominations. All of the allocations . . . have been respected. I am not so familiar with developments in Montana, but to the best of my knowledge the same fine spirit of cooperation has been manifest there since the organization of the Home Missions Council.

Our cities are rapidly spilling over with excess population, which is forming the multiplying suburban communities. Into these suburbs go the people from the various city churches, to minister to whom the various denominations are following with new churches. So there is happening before our eyes today the same competitive procedure which was so commonly approved yesterday and which is so universally condemned today as unethical. But here we are, inheritors of a system which apparently we cannot control. Denominational enterprises of far-reaching influence are dependent upon the gifts of the people of today and the gifts of their children of tomorrow. Therefore these Baptist people must be kept within the fold, a task that calls for a Baptist church in the new suburb! So the denominational executive views it; and who shall say that he is wrong? It may be recorded as fact, however, that many such men are not happy over the situation; yet they see no way to extricate us from it. Of course there is only one possible way out, now or in any near future, and that is the way of cooperative unity; and the comity plan.

The late Dr. Charles E. Goodall, who was Executive Secretary of the New Jersey Baptist Convention, was compelled to face this suburban problem as perhaps few others among Baptists, for into his territory came the swarms of New York City's excess population. Seeing no immediate means of escape, he nevertheless confessed that he felt immeasurably embarrassed by the apparent necessity of competitive denominationalism. His people were in its toils and seemed powerless to break away. But he and men of like responsibility in other denominations have not been minded to submit indefinitely to this system of competition. They have persisted in their faith in the possibility of cooperation. To this end, recent years have brought them into frequent conference, with promising results. Regarding this, Dr. Goodall said:

I and some other men of like responsibilities in our own and other denominations have the full support of our boards in prohibiting competition when organizing new churches in the suburban areas. Few, if any, new churches are planned for suburban areas without common agreements with the denominations. This is brought about through conference, and then the task of organizing a new church generally has the approval of the denominations operating in that area.

In the area of cooperative unity there has been considerable actual achievement as between and among the churches of local communities. In most such, we wish to believe, the churches are presenting a united front.

## Cooperative Unity, Federation, Organic Union

Yet cooperation is increasing, even among the larger denominational units, because of the work of local, state, and national councils of churches. In the perpetuation of a state of non-cooperation it is unnecessary to admit that Baptists are the chief of sinners; the facts reveal other large groups to be quite as clannish and sectarian. But public opinion is developing against competitive projects, and gives a corresponding hope that the day is at hand when we shall be able to set Kingdom interests above those of any particular denomination. There must arise the spirit of give-and-take, which alone can create the polity along whose lines united effort proceeds and cooperative unity is actualized as a dream at last come true. For this all men whose first concern is for the kingdom of God are today devoutly hoping.

Beyond cooperative unity, as a first step, lies federation as a second. Already there are many city and State federations of churches. For the most part these exist to promote what we have elected to call " cooperative unity," or united endeavor across denominational lines. Such is federated action rather than action by federated churches. Moreover, the church federations, so called, are quite uniformly prohibited from doing anything in the direction of reducing the number of churches in overchurched areas by uniting two or more in actual federation. Each denomination cooperating in the city or state federation is exceeding jealous lest it lose a single church, however weak, struggling, and impotent such may have become. When a genuine federation is effected it is almost invariably due to this very impotence. It were better to federate than to perish. Little wonder therefore that federations are not uniformly successful.

Nevertheless the pressure making for federations is

strong in a multitude of town and village communities. These most keenly feel the palsy of overchurching. This pressure has generated and advanced, during the present century, the community church movement. Churches of this type have arisen to the number of hundreds. In their rise they have followed no uniform pattern. Some are actual federations of two or more churches under the name " Community Church "; others are new creations, hoping to suck the waning life from local denominational groups, and yet others are simply denominational churches which have appropriated the " Community " name.

But strangely—not to say sorrowfully—the community church movement has really issued in another denomination. Inaugurated to solve the problem of overchurching, it has but added to the already existing confusion. The reason for this is not far to seek: A given community church had no connections in fellowship or service outside its own neighborhood. There were no denominational channels through which that kind of church could express its life or bear a broader witness. The felt need of fellowship and wider service drove these into associations, then into larger units, and finally into a country-wide organization with an appropriate program.

Genuine federation attacks the problem of overchurching. Taking cognizance of the fatal weakness of the community church movement, other lines of polity have been projected. To be concrete: A certain small town had three churches, one of which was contemplating the closing of its doors. This fact raised the question of federation of the three, and led on to conference and negotiations which came to a head in a federation as follows: The three groups were brought into a cooperative unity which preserved the identity of each. In the federation there was still a Baptist group, a Presbyterian group and a Congregational group. Each received and dismissed members, and, by missionary offerings and otherwise, maintained vital relations with its own denomination. In all local interests, however, they were one. They abandoned one church building, converted a second into a community house, and used the third for public worship, for the church school, and the like. Then too, they called one minister—who is still their minister—a very able man, of wide experience and outstanding success in large city parishes—who, incidentally, was of that denomination represented by the smallest group within this federation. The church is called " The Federated Church of ——."

This experiment has been uniformly successful for something like forty years. Consequently its type of federation has been copied. It has the great virtue of uniting the Christian forces of the community and at the same time maintaining vital connections with all the denominations concerned. One seeking membership in this church designates the group with which he wishes to affiliate, and subsequently is received in accordance with the practice and polity of that group. Manifestly such a church makes certain demands of the minister. For one thing, he cannot be denominationally-minded; he is pastor of all the people and as such must feed all. It will be necessary that he proclaim and live by those great fundamentals of the gospel that unite all in love and loyalty to Christ. Fortunately, a federation of all the Christian forces of the community, as in this case, will generally make it possible to secure a man sufficiently large in understanding and sympathy to meet the challenge indicated.

Yet another type of federation is spreading in certain

sections, namely, a federation under a denominational banner. Let us say that it shall be called " The Community Baptist Church of ——." Clearly it is designed to have a denominational tie-up; in this case with the Baptist denomination. It came into being because the Baptist was the one strong church of the neighborhood, the three others being weak and without influence or appeal. These were absorbed, so to speak. A new element herein is the working out of the principle of comity. There was agreement among the denominations concerned that, this federation being sanctioned, when conditions were otherwise Baptists would be agreeable to merger, say, into the Methodist church. Of course the local churches involved must be won to the proposed federation. The Baptist church in mind is established upon the open membership platform, in that it agreed to receive by letter all members from the federating groups, two of whom are non-immersing. However, it was consented that the church itself should baptize only by immersion, since only thus could happy relationship be retained with the denomination of which it is a part.

These federations, of whatever type, must be regarded as experiments; significant experiments, let it be granted. They are attempts to free us from the net of divisive denominationalism; and that is significant. And yet as experiments they are scarcely satisfactory to anyone. To the denominationalist they are churches adrift on the sea of disloyalty. To another they utterly fail in that they still do obeisance to sectarianism—save in the case of the Community Church—and it fails by creating another sect. We cannot bring our views to coincide with those of either critic. It should be clear that a way must be found to bring an end to competition and overcrowding.    So convinced, one will welcome any experiment which looks toward that end.[1]

Just as federation of local churches is a step farther removed from sectarianism than cooperative unity, so is also federation of denominations.    Recent times bear testimony that this latter is within the range of achievement; we note the United Church of Canada, which in 1925 federated Methodist, Presbyterian and Congregational bodies; and the approaches being made toward each other by different denominational groups within the United States.    Within Baptist circles the historic hesitancy prevails, though it is not without significance that in 1910 the Free Will Baptist denomination came in with Northern Baptists; and more recent years have witnessed agitation for a *rapproachement* between the latter and the Disciples of Christ.    Here are but straws indicating the direction in which the currents of thought are moving. Competitive denominationalism is, to say the least, being seriously questioned.

Our evaluation of these experiments in federation of denominations is rather negative.    As attempts to free ourselves from the embarrassments of competition, in an age which drives on toward a more inclusive cooperation in all fields of human endeavor, they are most commendable.    Nevertheless, we doubt their ultimate wisdom, particularly as they affect the five or six major denominations, including Baptists.    These groups are already large enough for effective work—which is the chief objective— and not infrequently so large as to make genuine unity difficult of maintenance.    Not only so, these major groups

---

[1] The Larger Parish Plan constitutes another promising experiment.    By it a number of churches are placed under the leadership of a competent staff of trained workers who carry a unified program for the whole parish.

are possessed of cherished histories, deeply rooted loyalties and well-established polities, which receive definite shock, if not actual destruction, when a federation is effected. So potent is this disturbance that it goes far to make the federation difficult to achieve, and once achieved, difficult to function, with a success seeming to justify its existence. To be sure, not much experimentation has been attempted, the United Church of Canada standing practically alone; and its history to date is not altogether convincing.

On the contrary, these considerations do not hold regarding the few score of small denominations. Alone, each of these is ineffective, without any great influence, and serving mostly to multiply divisions and increase waste. If these could find ways to federate with the major groups of their respective choices, it would be greatly to enhance the potency of the forces that make for the coming of the Kingdom. Baptists can ill afford not so to extend their labors as to bring into federation those smaller bodies which are near of kin in life, doctrine and polity.

The foregoing discussion makes clear that federation lies close to organic union, in fact has a tendency to issue in the latter, as we have seen. Throughout the latter half century agitation for a united church has been effective in winning many converts. The solidarity of that world of unrighteousness which is in unending opposition to the church has become so manifest that multitudes can see naught but defeat for a divided church. Moreover, movements toward consolidation and cooperation are a notable characteristic of the times. All these considerations have been working together to make good men in all denominations impatient with divisions that work for impotency.

## Cooperative Unity, Federation, Organic Union

To find the army of the King of Kings hopelessly divided in the face of a united foe, is a condition that rubs raw the sensitized Christian conscience. The situation seems not only tragic, but so sinful as to be beyond the pale of divine pardon.

Out of the Edinburgh Missionary Conference of 1910 came the expressed hope for a world conference of the churches of Christ to explore the whole area which lay between division and unity. In the autumn of the same year the Protestant Episcopal Church in the United States gave attention to the matter, furthering it by the appointment of a committee charged to work toward a "World Conference on Faith and Order." This move was seconded by various other groups during the next decade, so that a preliminary meeting was convened in Geneva in 1920, wherein some seventy church bodies, representative of many nations, were present. This conference definitely forwarded the World Conference idea, which eventuated, in the summer of 1927, at Lausanne, Switzerland, seventeen years after its inauguration.

In the meantime came the World War. During the fury of that storm various branches of the church universal made appeals for peace. In the same vein the Federal Council of the Churches of Christ in America put forth the idea of a modern ecumenical council, an idea which met ready endorsement by Christians in Switzerland, Great Britain, Hungary, Holland and other nations. In consequence there was launched in August, 1920, at Geneva, a movement looking toward, "The Universal Conference of the Churches of Christ on Life and Work." In April of the next year the general committee, meeting in Peterborough, England, changed the name to "The Universal Conference on Life and Work." This conference was finally convened in Stockholm during the summer of 1925. The World Council of Churches, organized in 1948, now embraces 165 denominations.

If out of all such conferences there came only a better understanding, their value is beyond our power to compute. Had they been maintained across the centuries, divisions would undoubtedly have been fewer and there would have been an inestimable gain for the working forces that expand the empire of the Christ.

From 1925 to 1959 is not a long time, yet what vast progress has been made! Not only have state, national and world organizations been created and 165 denominations (or Churches) enlisted in the Ecumenical movement, but many conferences of world significance have witnessed a growing understanding and have established an annual budget of more than a million dollars for the promotion of an extensive and growing program. After more than nineteen centuries, Christians in all parts of the world are awakening to the realization of that spirit of oneness and sympathy which permeated and motivated the Christians of the first century.

To students of polity these world conferences reveal a most interesting fact, namely, that their respective programs are compelled to give attention largely, if not exclusively, to " life and work." They cannot touch polity; it is the exposed nerve of denominationalism. The consideration that really matters, the Master's kind of life and deed, can become elemental in a world-conference program; whereas those lesser matters of group practice are too hot to handle. The Lausanne and Evanston Conferences could spend days talking about the life of felfowship and love in Christ, but they could not assemble their delegates about his table.

That revelation may be disturbing, even nauseating.
And yet it is well to have the true conditions brought into
the light, if for no other reason than this, that it shows
men how distant is the goal they seek and what are the
obstacles that lie in the way. It makes very clear how
significant is this man-made, experience-born fabric of
polity.

Those who feel embarrassment, even to the point of
shame, because of their inheritance in competitive denominationalism, ought to temper with caution any questions
they raise regarding the desirability of one organically
unified church. The movement in that direction is too
noble in its spirit, and is sponsored by too excellent a portion of the church, to be treated in other than serious vein.
If God is leading toward organic union as the sublime
cure for our divisive ills, few would wish to be found in
opposition. And yet we do question the validity of the
movement. Manifestly God has not created men of one
mind, or after one mold. In the realm of religion they
do not see, or think, or feel as one—a fact which may
reveal divine wisdom. Many angles of vision bring under
the caption of knowledge every square inch of the surrounded mountain. By the same token many men of
many minds apprehend the greater truth that is in Christ
Jesus our Lord.

Frankly, we are unconvinced that the organic union of
the church universal is desirable, even though it were
possible. Its very size, when contemplated, appears certain to be unwieldly and awkward. It would stand a
chance of getting in its own way and stumbling over its
own feet. Moreover, how such a world-organism would
keep the circulation of real life-blood moving to the tips
of its ponderous limbs seems so problematic as to be

terrifying. We cannot possibly enthuse over the prospect of this super-dinosaur. And, too, history seems to vindicate our comparative indifference; for was there not once an organically united Church?

With all the zeal which our age manifests for large-size units and for ever-widening spheres of cooperation, it is yet very fearful of anything that looks like standardization of life. Modern industry has tried out this philosophy of standardization, and as a result has on its hands a sizable rebellion. Men refuse to be run into the same mold, or to be converted into machines; it seems contrary to basic human nature and its genius. And would not an organically unified Church tend to standardize the religious phases of life? Would it not tell men what to think? Would it not desire to prescribe their conduct in minutiæ? Would it not put handcuffs upon all man's freedoms? We should fear it. Our surmise is that should the ideal of a united Church of Christ be made actual today, within five hundred years there would be another Reformation, whose reverberation of protest would shake the whole earth.

However, should the coming years make clear that the great Head of the church is leading us on toward an organic union of all denominations, Baptists will surely be found not the least zealous of those who meet about the conference table to project that union and its policies. Through all the years the pole-star in their sky has been to do the Master's bidding, and in this case they could be counted on not to falter. Once at that table where Christian statesmen were conferring, they would have an important contribution to make to the life and polity of such a united church. First of all, they would insist upon a recognition of the full competency of every soul in matters of religion. This principle, they would urge, must be accepted as basic, and to be directive in all the deliberations.

There would be ample risk of violation of this principle. Freedom of the individual to order his own religious life, without coercion at any point, is endangered as polity and organization become more complex. The drag toward monopoly is strong. There can be no authoritative priesthood, no interference by the state, no curtailing of soul liberty anywhere. Then too, the local congregations throughout the proposed united church would need to be hedged about, guaranteeing a large measure of local autonomy. Churches must have the sacred right to blunder as well as to achieve. They may be offered wisdom and leadership, but must be secure in their right to reject both. In other words, the local churches must be established in that measure of freedom which permits competent souls to accept responsibility, develop initiative, and largely share as free partners in Kingdom projects. Such matters as the time, place, and manner of administering the ordinances, for instance, might be left to local churches, as also the details of organization and polity.

When we sit down to think through the problem of creating the United Church of Christ in all the earth, we discover ourselves meeting the same general issue as that which confronted the fathers who wrought the Constitution of the United States of America, namely, how to secure a just and proper balance between State and Federal governments. That is the identical problem facing those who contemplate church union on a world-wide basis. The major question is how to maintain at the same time sufficient centralization of power to create a working

P  [ 213 ]

unity and sufficient decentralization to guarantee life in tip and toe of the institution. If and when the time comes to sit in conference for the creation of the United Church, the Baptist delegates will undoubtedly constitute a " bloc " doing battle for the largest possible measure of decentralization and local autonomy.

And now abide cooperative unity, federation, and organic union, but the greatest of these is ——? As each has its advocates so each has its very great virtues. However, we cast our vote for cooperative unity; but hasten to add, providing the other two are to operate to lift the curse of overchurching and sectarian competition. We believe that, on the whole, best results would be achieved by cooperative unity, as follows: by the processes of federation and organic union let the denominations be reduced, say to five, whose lines shall extend through all the earth, but always in obeisance to a plan of comity agreed to by the five. Let there be established a congress whose function it shall be to work out cooperatively programs of education, social service, evangelism, missionary enterprise and all the rest. Such a congress would serve to keep the denominations in step, to prevent overlapping in some areas and neglect of others, and generally to promote understanding and good-will. The existent National Council of the Churches of Christ in the United States of America might constitute itself the congress in question, or at least provide a working model therefor, together with much accumulated wisdom.

Five denominations (we arbitrarily state the number) in close cooperation would possess all the advantages, it seems to us, of organic union and none of its disadvantages. Organic union aims to provide unified counsel and a unified front as the church makes its impact upon the non-Christian phases of society. It would write the death warrant of overlapping, competition, and all the other ills of sectarianism. And finally, it would bring to the individual and the local church a new sense of strength, born of the solidarity of the forces of Christ with which they are integrating their lives.

But the cooperative unity of five denominations as proposed would be able to achieve the same ends. Cooperation through a congress, or council, with its functioning boards and committees, would provide the united front and the effective impact. It would gradually bring an end to sectarian competitions in both local and world-wide fields; the way would be that of comity. It would bring to the individual Christian and local church the desired sense of strength; each would be a vital part of one of the five active divisions that together would constitute the army of the Lord. In short, no advantage accrues to organic union which does not seem possible of achievement through cooperative unity. On the other hand cooperative unity proposes a polity void of many ills indigenous to organic union. For instance, the former provides immediately for a large measure of decentralization; at least there are five centers rather than one. And by so much it escapes the paralyzing effects of conformity, to secure which coercion lies too close at hand for comfort. Under a polity of cooperation large acreage is given individual initiative to run and graze and perchance kick up its heels. Cooperation provides a possible freedom difficult to secure under oneness of organization. The history of Christianity is eloquent concerning this difficulty. And freedom must be held at all cost, for out of it come the many new discoveries and surmises which keep alive and make for progress. By no means the least of the virtues promised by cooperative unity is that of healthful rivalry, *friendly* rivalry let us urge. Five great denominations working side by side would develop their respective procedures and polities, and evolve each its own characteristic genius, thereby rivaling each other in good works; the end result of which would give a greatly enriched Christianity. In the suggested organic union we fear the lurking malaria of self-satisfaction and perfect contentment, the end of which is death. Nothing is better designed to drain off the stagnant waters of that swamp than an active rivalry such as the suggested cooperative unity provides.

One final consideration. Cooperative unity would give rise to a polity which takes cognizance of wide differences among men; differences in opinions, in interpretations, in tastes, in cultural backgrounds. To bring all these into one fold, wherein each is to be joyous in his religious expression, we confess seems a practical impossibility. This might, conceivably, be achieved by a generous use of either opiate or intoxicant. But a cooperative unity among a few great denominations need not resort to such extremes. Each individual or local church has five different groups from which to choose one composed of kindred spirits; failing in this, the one concerned is most likely too peculiar to fellowship with any save himself, and may, therefore, be ignored.

No, we shall not attempt to name the five denominations. However, two might well be the Eastern and Western Catholic Churches, and three composed of present-day Protestant bodies, one representing each of three types of polity, espicopal, presbyterial and congregational. Within these respective frameworks all could conceivably find a home, at once congenial, and effective for the world-wide cooperative enterprise on behalf of Jesus Christ—whom we all fain would love and serve.

Someone, perhaps a Baptist, is sure to arise and quote, " Physician, heal thyself; whatever we have heard, etc." —and thereby dismiss the whole matter. But it cannot be so glibly and flippantly dismissed. The problem of competitive denominationalism will not be shouted down, however insistent the heckler. It is before us and a solution must be found. A solution will be found; for a divisive denominationalism is a leopard that must either be made radically to change its spots and its nature, or it will devour Christianity itself. By the spirit of the age its death has been decreed and they are legion who are already beating the bush with rifle in hand. Denominationalism as we have known it is certain to be a trophy hung in a museum of antiquities in some not-far distant tomorrow.

We shall not pursue the figure further. It remains that a way out of the pit of competitive denominationalism is going to be dug. That seems to be perfectly assured. Our suggestion is that we begin digging where we are, proceed practically in accordance with cooperation, federation, and union, in the hope of final emergence into the free cooperation of a few major denominations.

### Topics for Group Discussion

1. Think of some small community known to the group; a community manifestly overchurched. How would the group remedy the situation?

2. Resolved, that cooperative unity among the denominations is an end more to be desired than either some type of federation, or organic union.

[ 217 ]

3. Given a rapidly developing suburban area, adjacent to a great city, would it be desirable to prevent over-churching? If so, just how may that end be achieved?

4. Let us suppose a community of seven hundred persons and four churches: Should the three weaker consent to disband, on condition that the Baptist church would undertake to minister to all, would the group recommend an open membership policy for this church? (By "open membership" is meant the reception of members by letter from non-immersing churches.)

5. Should Baptists indefinitely support mission boards that continue to use funds to keep alive weak churches in overchurched communities?

6. What are the weaknesses inherent in the Community Church movement?

### Books Worth Consulting

Beers, G. Pitt, *Ministry to Turbulent America*. The Judson Press, Philadelphia, 1957.

Bilheimer, Robert S., *The Quest for Christian Unity*. The Association Press, New York, 1952.

Garrison, Winfred E., *The Quest and Character of a United Church*. The Abingdon Press, Nashville, 1957.

Handy, Robert T., *We Witness Together*. The Friendship Press, New York, 1956.

Trueblood, Elton, *The Common Venture of Life*. Harper and Brothers, New York, 1949.

World Council of Churches, Evanston Assembly. *The Christian Hope and the Task of the Church*. Harper and Brothers, 1954.

## PRACTICAL SUGGESTIONS

1. If your own town, or some town near-by, is an illustration of an impoverished religious life due to over-churching and sectarian divisions, lead your group to study the situation with a view to doing something about it.

2. Inspire your class to seek opportunities to cooperate with similar groups in churches other than Baptist in enterprises that look toward a more Christian community life.

3. Encourage the group to ascertain what movement, if any, is now looking toward other world conferences, when and where such will likely convene, and what agenda are being proposed. If sufficient interest develops the group may become the means of sending one or more delegates to such a conference.

# XIII

## THE KINGDOM AND THE CHURCHES

### The Kingdom

The precise phrase, " kingdom of God," does not occur in the Old Testament, though the idea is there. A few references will indicate its prevalence: 1 Chronicles 29: 11 —" Thine is the kingdom, O Lord, and thou art exalted as head above all "; Psalm 22: 28—" The kingdom is the Lord's and he is the governor among the nations "; Psalm 45: 6—" The sceptre of thy kingdom is a right sceptre "; Psalm 145: 11—" They shall speak of the glory of thy kingdom, and talk of thy power "; Daniel 2: 44—"And in the days of these kings shall the God of heaven set up a kingdom which shall never be destroyed . . . it shall break in pieces and consume all these kingdoms and it shall stand forever and ever." Though the idea is everywhere imbedded in the Old Scriptures, its content is by no means uniform. It is an idea describing a plainly marked development curve, passing from the crassly material to the highly spiritual, from the narrowly national to the inclusively universal. Merely to note this development suffices our present purpose, which is to indicate that we are dealing with a living and hence a changing idea.

The predominant strain in the idea, however, was physical; there was contemplated an earthly kingdom wherein God should reign, either in person or through one whom he should especially anoint. A dominant conception made this kingdom synonymous with the Jewish theocracy as it then existed. With the development of ethical insight, however, it was no longer possible to claim that God actually ruled in that particular governmental institution. The great prophets spilled that content out of the idea when they cried out against every conceivable kind of unrighteousness that shot through and through the life of the theocracy. They thought the time was coming when God surely would redeem Israel and establish a righteous reign; but when and how was their problem. That such was central in the purpose of Jehovah they never doubted. With all but unanimity these towering religious leaders reiterate the hope of a coming Kingdom of righteousness, one essentially God's kingdom. Whether it should be set up by Israel as son of God, or by one of the ancient prophets returning with a divine commission to establish it, or by some other kind of messiah, or by the coming of Jehovah himself to make actual his benevolent purpose, was a matter of wide divergence of opinion. Nevertheless, the conviction that the people, God's chosen people, would be established by him in some righteous social order was not among things questioned.

The Syrian and Roman dominations served to give life and effectiveness to the idea; God must provide one who should break in pieces the yoke of the oppressor and destroy his rule. The most prominent phase of the hope thus took the definite form of a divine reestablishment of the Davidic line and the extension of its sway over all other nations and peoples. It proposed conversion by means of national lordship. Thus revitalized, the idea gave birth to the apocalypses, most of which prophesy the ascendency of the house of David, under peculiar, divine endowment that would empower it to bring all into subjection. The Book of Daniel is the best-known of these apocalypses in the older scriptures, and is a narrowly nationalistic writing. Uprisings had been attempted under Judas Maccabæus and other leaders in the belief that such would serve to summon the Messiah and initiate the reign of Jehovah so long expected. There were " zealots " of differing hue, but all alike in that they were loyalist to the core—the one hundred per cent. nationalists of their time. The Messiah whom they expected was to be a national leader, appointed to extend the sway of Jerusalem over all the earth.

With too few exceptions—like Simeon and Anna who " waited for the kingdom "—this was the kingdom-idea whose noise filled the world into which our Lord was born. On every hand were these organizations of zealots, men with a nationalistic complex, who served to fan the fires of nationalism, and hatred for the oppressor. They marched under the banner of patriotism and as openly as they dared agitated for revolt in the name of Jehovah and country. They constituted a Jingoist element within the population, who, it has been assumed, had the clandestine backing of the influential Pharisaic party. Rome was noticeably worried and irritated by the unsettled state of affairs and was keeping a close watch on every movement symptomatic of revolt. Long experience in dealing with subject peoples had taught her the exceeding inflammability of patriotism when compounded with religion—as was notably the case with this " chosen people." They looked for the direct intervention of God to break the back of the Roman rule and to establish in its stead his heavenly kingdom. The whole situation was decidedly tense. And alas! there was no great prophet in the land to bring the steadying influence of a vitally religious message, to give a spiritual interpretation of the kingdom hope.

At this juncture came John the Baptist, a voice crying in the wilderness. The times were ripe for the lifting of a prophetic voice. It is no accident that " all Jerusalem and Judea " went to the banks of the Jordan to hear his message. He was proclaiming the dawn of a new age, for proper living in which men should repent of their sins and seek the ways of Jehovah. As many as gave evidence of such repentance he was baptizing, as a sign and seal of the new life purpose and the readiness for citizenship in a new age. *This moral element* is John's distinct contribution to current thought regarding the kingdom of God. It is significant that certain dominant ecclesiastical groups did not appreciate this emphasis. Their members were most desirous of a new era, but not of the kind that demanded of them anything like repentance. For this unseemly attitude toward his message the prophet condemned them in scathing terms; he denounced them as vipers and as whited sepulchers. His passionate ethical sense led him to castigate even his ruler, Herod Antipas, for his wanton manner of life. This course cost him his life; but not until he had won and baptized his great Successor.

Though John made ethical advance over contemporaneous thought concerning the new age, he did not clearly break with that thought at other important points. He held that the reign of Jehovah was at hand, that the Messiah had arrived, who would reestablish the kingdom of David in unbelievable glory. His method would be cataclysmic. He was here as one with a fan in his hand, prepared to burn the chaff and rescue the precious grain, to separate the impenitent and unrighteous from those who had paid heed to his own message of repentance. In other words, the Messiah had come to institute the great and terrible day of judgment and thus usher in the reign of the righteous God.

At this critical juncture John was cast into prison—and later beheaded—and Jesus of Nazareth whom he had pointed out as the Promised One took up the burden of the Kingdom. And a burden it indeed was, for in many respects the times were "out of joint." Expectancy ran as a flood-tide. And what a grievous content was in that expectation! Tragedy was in the offing for the One who had come to change that content. The single hopeful element therein was that which John had contributed, that is to say, his call for a righteous life. That much, at least, was spiritual; but beyond that the hope was baldly physical and crassly temporal.

In certain respects John was indeed a forerunner for the Messiah. He had captured the masses and electrified them with expectancy of the imminent reign of God. He had sounded, strong and clear, the ethical note; in this regard being a true successor of the great prophets of bygone days. He had recognized and introduced the Messiah, one greater than himself whose shoe-latchet he was not worthy to unloose. In other respects John had scarcely helped the situation. He had crystalized the idea of a physical, earthly kingdom, which was to be set up after the fashion predicted by the apocalyptists. Neither of these ideas bulked large in the mind and purpose of Christ, and so constituted danger-points as he went out upon his mission. Little wonder that John, languishing in Herod's prison, should have become disappointed in him whom he had declared to be the long-expected Deliverer. He was neither instituting the judgment nor establishing anew the throne of David. Jesus' reply to John's deputation of inquiry, couched in language of tenderness and respect, is both reassuring and significant: " Go and show John again those things which you hear and see; the blind receive their sight, and the lame walk, the lepers are cleansed and the deaf hear, the dead are raised up and the poor have the gospel preached unto them. And blessed is he who shall not be offended in me." There follows the Master's high evaluation of John and his ministry, one of the most eloquent tributes ever paid by one to his predecessor. (Matt. 11 : 7-15.)

The significance of that message sent to John must not be overlooked. It lays bare at once Jesus' conception of the kingdom of God and the method he proposed for its establishment. The Kingdom was essentially non-physical; it had to do with the kind of life one lived; and it must be established by means of love within the heart expressing itself in terms of kindly and generous service to one's fellowmen. It is patent that this view of the Kingdom was a thousand miles from that which was current among the people. But in the forty days in the wilderness our Lord had thought through and fought through the whole matter. In that retreat his vision came to crystal clearness that God's kingdom is preeminently spiritual, and that the one and only way to grow that Kingdom is by the slow processes of the lovely, Godlike life which makes its continuing and constant impact upon the lives of others until they catch its divine spark. Such a life might turn out to be that of the patiently suffering Servant, as visioned by Isaiah, yet for that end he had come—if so the Father willed. In that decision he set his face toward the cross. A disappointed nation would kill him.

With clearness of mind and fixity of purpose the Son of God came forth from his wilderness seclusion heralding the gospel of the kingdom of God; good news about the reign of God in the hearts of men and their affairs. He came reiterating the essential message of John, the message of repentance. " Repent, repent! " he called to men everywhere. Like his forerunner, he announced the imminence of the Kingdom, but passed beyond him to declare its actual presence now. Like John, he declared the new life to be the badge of entrance to that Kingdom, but, as we have noted, his idea of the Kingdom thus entered was foreign to the thought of the fiery prophet who had stirred the passions of the multitudes on the banks of the Jordan. He employed John's language but not John's meanings; in other phrase, he was filling full of richer thought the words that had resounded in the wilderness.

To any student of the Master's life, message, and work it is certain that his major concern was for what he termed the kingdom of God, or kingdom of heaven. From the outset he preached the Kingdom. It was the major note in all his teaching. His beautiful and majestic parables are in illustration of some phase or characteristic of it. In the superlative wording of the Model Prayer he frames at the center its undying welfare. In exact language he urges, " Seek ye first the kingdom of God, and God's kind of righteousness, and all these other things will be added unto you." Exactly so. Most of that for which the human heart rightly longs will come in the natural course of events; but the Kingdom?—it must be held at the center of the purposive life, whose logical fruit will be, " all these things." The kingdom of heaven is to constitute, for the disciple of Christ, the dominant and dominating ideal, the ideal that integrates and holds together the entire life; the ideal that gives it purpose and drive, balance and poise; the ideal that makes a life fruitfully significant in the Father's eyes.

With the certainty of the centrality of the kingdom of heaven in the message of the Great Teacher, we turn to an analytic study of that creative idea. We note at the outset that it anchors its interest in the individual. The individual is the microcosm with which the Kingdom primarily concerns itself. It never transcends him nor in any wise neglects him. He is the superlative value with which it has to do. He is, in the fulness of his life, its alpha and omega, beginning and end. The fruitage to the growing of which it is dedicated is a certain inner quality of mind and heart; a result secured by orienting his life in the sphere of faith and trust in God.

A casual survey of, say, Matthew's Gospel, will vindicate this primacy of the individual. We see the Master himself in the rôle of striking individuality as he visits the Jordan, listens attentively to John's preaching and decides to accept his baptism. His retirement into the wilderness carries forward the intense personal drama. Victor in that struggle for personal certainty and assurance, he emerged from his lonely sojourn crying to men, "Repent, for the kingdom of heaven is at hand!" a message to individuals, obviously. The so-called Sermon on the Mount deals with the individual and the quality of life that will open to him the Kingdom. The Beatitudes, whose phrases float like banners in air, herald those personal virtues and elements of character which the reign of God both demands and begets. And so on, chapter after chapter, to the very end runs *the individual strain,* in every teaching: the parable of the Mote and the Beam; the Call to the Narrow Gate; the teaching about good and evil trees; Peter's confession; the casuistry of him who comes to the altar shouting, "Corban!"; the enjoining of forgiveness; the parable of the Laborers and their individualistic contracts; the injustice of the Wicked Husbandman. In every case the individual is made the center of interest and concern, the Rome toward which all Kingdom highways converge.

However, this does not imply a lack of social concern, which is often set forth as the logical inference. On the contrary, the most potent social outreach is indicated as both necessary and inevitable. Despite what we have said in the foregoing paragraphs, there is a sense in which there is no such thing as an individual. No man lives to himself, neither can he. Even the fictitious Robinson Crusoe, whose fascination lies in his tragic isolation, must have his man Friday and his goat. The Master's portrayal of the kingdom of heaven always put the man and his neighbor in the same frame. In it I always live with my brother, and the roots of our lives grow together inextricably. Every man is a Siamese Twin—to his hurt does he injure or neglect the other. That is to say, the individual is born into and lives in a social world; for such was he created, and in such the Kingdom calls him to grow into fulness of stature. Therefore to neglect the most far-reaching social implications is to emasculate the gospel of our Lord beyond recognition.

The dominant note in his preaching is worthy of quoting again, "Repent, for the kingdom of heaven is at hand." At the same time he was explaining, "the kingdom of heaven is in you" ("among you"). Clearly, his thought was that the Kingdom is present. Being essentially spiritual, it is not something that is to come, but it is already here. It is present wherever and whenever the mind and purpose of God have become the mind and purpose of a man, wherever and whenever the qualities in the mind and heart of the Father begin to show themselves in the mind and heart of his child. There and then is the Kingdom revealed as here. As such it is " in " the individual and at the same time " among " a group of such regenerate individuals. One is in the Kingdom when the Kingdom gets into him, when its impulses and passions become operative in his manner of living. But such impulses and passions cannot be confined; they inevitably overflow the rim of life and spill their contagion to the group. As the water in the well filled the old oaken bucket both inside and out, so is the life of the individual filled by the kingdom of heaven.

Viewing that Kingdom to be now in the world—as did Jesus who gave vitality and dynamic to the Kingdom idea—we think it true to his thought to say that the kingdom of God has always been in the world, even from the beginning. Wherever the sway of the loving Father has approximated completeness in the life of a man, there was the Kingdom manifest in power. If the Kingdom's borders had been very narrow hitherto, it was because few had entered it by permitting it to enter them. Hitherto they had been so blinded by unseeing teachers that they could not recognize it when it knocked at their very doors. By false leaders they had been called to wait for, hope for, and expect some elaborate physical establishment, an earthly kingdom of the Davidic type magnified. Thus passionately expecting some régime out of heaven from God, they were unable to apprehend the truth that God's kingdom must grow up in and among his people, a kingdom indigenous to their own life. It is this Kingdom

Q

that God sent his beloved Son to reveal to men, this Kingdom to which he dedicated his mature thought, and in the interests of which he gave all the fulness of his life. The Kingdom was indeed " at hand," with significance, when he came, for he was destined to fill all the world with the glory of its challenge.

A spiritual kingdom of heaven, as the Master conceived it, was not only past and present; it had a future as well. The hope of great expansion ran on down across all the years. The Kingdom of the past and present but represented the acorn stage, the mighty oak belonged to the future. As yet it is only a mustard-seed; in the to-morrows it will grow to be a tree giving food and shelter to the multitudes. It was future in precisely the sense that all that grows and develops is future. Its coming will mark all the stages of blade, ear, and full corn in the ear. Its expansion will be like the working of yeast in a batch of dough: quiet, pervasive, full of vitality, life-changing. No noise and fury will attend its coming, no portents may be expected concerning which men shout, " Lo here and lo there! " Then, too, the Kingdom's futurity stretched into the world beyond death. In fact, that world would witness the final fruitage, the consummation of what was here in the processes of becoming. For a spiritual kingdom of God cannot be limited by such physical boundaries as death and the grave. It adheres primarily in the quality of life which under divine nurture has been achieved by the soul. These qualities constitute the wings of glory on which it fares forth into immortal life beyond the borders of the present world. In a word, the Kingdom is universal in purpose, as universal as the purpose of God; its actuality is limited only by the limits of its sway set by men unwilling to grant its sway in their own hearts. The Kingdom is the reign of God in the lives of men.

Every earthly kingdom has its citizens, likewise the kingdom of heaven. They are those who have performed the rites of initiation which it demands. Chiefly these constitute a foreswearing of allegiance to the world and a declaration of loyalty to God's rule in their lives. It constitutes a pledge to follow the Christ who himself has walked in all the ways of the Kingdom and filled to the full all its requirements. Once in the Kingdom, by self-commitment to him whom the Father has anointed Lord thereof, the righteous life becomes the goal of the citizen. "Seek ye first the kingdom of God and his quality of righteousness," is the call that canalizes his energies and lifts all his endeavors to a high potential. Thus religion comes to flower in the ethical life, in quality like that of the beloved Son, master in the kingdom of heaven. In a very real sense, therefore, coming to Christ is equivalent to coming into the Kingdom; truly so if coming to him means the hearty espousal for one's self of his manner of living. He embodied the Kingdom in himself, and every right worthy citizen aims to do the same thing.

Heaven's Kingdom, like every other, has its enemies. They are those who for many reasons are not agreeable to the reign of God either in their own hearts or in the world of human affairs. Some are enemies by indifference, some by active opposition. Some are too sluggish to assume the responsibilities of the Kingdom, others are too preoccupied to hear its challenge. Yet others are hostile to all for which the Kingdom stands; they oppose the reign of God in any sector, most likely because such augurs interference with their own selfish ends and their own particular form of special privilege. Concerning these the Master's counsel in the parable of the Tares is interesting: Let the wheat and the tares, the good and the evil, grow together until the harvest. Here, as often, he does not speak in the absolute; as if teaching non-interference with evil men and their plans. What he does counsel is that sons of the Kingdom must not devote their major energies to opposing these, but rather that they give first attention to those constructive enterprises that aim to enlarge the Father's reign. And after all, is not the evil that men plan most effectively thwarted by the bulk of good which they must first overcome? If so—as we believe—the wisdom of the Master is but once more vindicated. Who has not witnessed with what great folly some good men passionately oppose the forces of evil, only to find themselves so exhausted thereby as to have nothing left for constructive endeavor in the Kingdom of righteousness? It is just this that our Lord warns against—and of course not against effective attempts to undo the plans of the forces of evil. Increasing study of the life and ministry of Jesus brings one to the awareness of a certain even tenor of moderation in all that he was and did. Extremes he studiously avoided. In the parable of the Tares, he urges moderation and a sane balance between the primary work of enlarging the borders of the Kingdom and that of opposing its enemies.

For it must never be forgotten that the glory of the Kingdom is its fruitfulness; what it bears in terms of the ennobled and enriched lives of its sons or citizens. "In this is your Father glorified, that ye bear much fruit," is the high note in the parable of the Vine. Barrenness is contemplated in sorrow. What a pathetic note is struck in the parable of the Soils, when one after another fails to yield a good crop! The soil much trodden, that filled with stones, and that preempted by thorns, proves in turn to be merely a devourer of good seed; worse than useless. Not so with "the good ground," for it yields from sixty- to an hundred-fold. That is the final test of a soil—and the superlative test of a citizen of the Kingdom. He is like a tree planted which bears the delicious fruit of the righteous life in every season. Failing in this he has failed in all. For by and through such fruit only is there hope of winning the world to the kingdom of heaven.

## THE CHURCH

The first churches took their rise out of the Kingdom ideal and the Kingdom passion. Through the transcendently divine personality of our Lord this ideal had caught fire in the hearts of men. His passion for the Kingdom had begun to flow down through human society as a social force. And like every social force, it soon created for itself an embodiment in the form of a social institution. That institution was an organized fellowship of disciples, a Christian church. It was born of the gospel of the Kingdom, the gospel of our Lord Jesus Christ, and was dedicated wholly to the interests of that gospel. Every such church was to constitute itself a miniature kingdom of God, its members citizens, living by its laws and producing in their lives the fruits of the Father's reign in their hearts.

Of some such *ecclesia,* or organized fellowship, devoted to the forwarding of the work he had begun, Jesus had dreamed. Looking forward to its coming he had now and again planted a seed in the heart of a disciple, and had quietly nurtured its germination, assured that when the times were ripe a church would result. And just so it came to pass. For the erection of such a church he had given no blue-print and written no polity therefor. He trusted rather to the genius of the Kingdom movement which he was launching to create for itself a suitable institutional medium for the effective expression of its life. Precisely this is what the student of the documents —the New Testament writings—discovers.

Now the Baptist churches have consciously aimed at the reproduction of this initial process in their own origin, growth, and ministry. We are unable to say that the ideal has been actualized in every instance, yet on the whole the guiding genius of the New Testament has been fully relied upon. At least the desire to submit to that guidance, as they understand it, has been continuous among Baptists. And wherever the New Testament has been free to direct, there has eventuated a church, or churches, commendably dedicated to the gospel of the kingdom of God as interpreted by our Lord, supreme Head of the church universal.

Let us view the Baptist churches—considering particularly their structural polity—as they relate themselves to this Kingdom and its good news which Christ heralded. Now in studying about this our initial discovery was that the Kingdom sets the individual at the center. With this basic fact the doctrine of soul-competency, espoused by Baptists, exactly comports. The individual's growth into the fulness of life as it was in the Master is the first and primary function of the church. Their polity, as we have seen in an earlier chapter, aims at the nurturing and safeguarding of his competency, and the guidance of his growth as a free son of God. Like the kingdom of God which a church would embody in miniature, the individual is the beginning and the end of its concern. It must give to the world men and women of the Christ pattern and mold, those attaining something of his stature, or admit that its ministry is abortive.

Though centering attention upon the individual and his entrance upon the way of life with his Lord, a church of the Baptist order aims to generate in its membership the social passion. If it is actually to live up to its charter as a replica of the kingdom of God, it must manifest that Kingdom's concern for the health of human society and the general welfare of men everywhere. This constitutes every church in the most inclusive sense a missionary institution. It must aim to reach out with a long arm—whose hand gives the touch of moral and religious health—to its environing world. Only as the individual joins in such a vital outreach can he claim to be like his Lord.

With a view to the enriching of the social passion of the churches we pause to consider the interpretation of a difficult passage, " Ye are a colony of heaven " (Phil. 3 : 20, Moffatt). A church of Christ, a colony of heaven! Contemplate that idea, particularly how a given colony extends its influence. Maintaining its own solidarity and its loyalty to the language and customs of the homeland, it begins to make its impacts upon the indigenous society. By patience, persistence, tact and grace it wins its way, and finally possesses those among whom it has come to dwell. Every missionary is such a colonist; but so also is every church-member. And what is more, every church is a " colony of heaven," located in a certain community for the express purpose of winning that community for the Kingdom. A heaven-sent colony, charged to be true to heavenly ideals and life, appointed to speak the language and work the works of heaven, until all whom it may contact are won to that manner of living for which the colony is advocate and exemplar. What it would mean to our world if every church did constitute an actual colony of heaven! Might we cherish such a high aim for every Baptist church.

As our Lord, empowered in the wilderness, returned to the quiet villages of Galilee crying, " Repent, and enter the Kingdom "; so would each church call to men. A dominant note in its ministry must be evangelistic, a regnant passion in its heart to win folks as disciples of Christ and children of the Kingdom. The New Testament churches were thus alert bearers of the message of repentance and the graces of life that await those who enter the Kingdom. To this message the Baptist churches have been remarkably true. Their polity has made way for a passionate evangelism; and thereby they have grown. It has constituted a chief mode and method of impact upon the world; and in so far it is greatly to their credit. That they have not infrequently left undone other ministries of equal merit is to be regretted, yet it may be said in extenuation that no single branch of the church universal can claim a program which embodies the full gospel ministry. Incidentally, this may be one of the very best excuses for some multiplicity of denominations; such means a multiplicity of emphasis, and hence the hope of the presentation of the whole gospel of Christ to men.

Thinking through the whole Kingdom ideal with Christ, we are established in a spiritual interpretation thereof. We have been led by his spirit to eschew all physical and apocalyptic interpretations, and look rather for that reign of God in the hearts of men which comes as quietly as a summer breeze whose kiss is registered on the cheek, but concerning which one may not say whence it cometh or whither it goeth. Truth demands that it be written that the Baptist churches, like most others, have not always given a witness wholly consistent with the Master's interpretation; they have sometimes sat with folded hands waiting for something to happen. But in the Sunday school movement, from the beginning of which they have not been the least potent of its exponents, a divine hand planted the seed of better things. Out of that is growing the present-day programs of Christian education, which assume that the kingdom of God is spiritual. Consequently beginning is made at the cradle to throw about the child a religious conception of the world wherein the Father God is growing his Kingdom and of which he wishes each to be a citizen and subject. In such an atmosphere is sought to germinate and nurture the Kingdom in the growing life of the child, to set his feet early in the ways of life dictated by Christ, the Lord of the Kingdom. Modern Christian education holds the Kingdom to be essentially non-physical, and that as such it must be grown " within " and " among " the people; thus taking seriously and wisely the pronouncement of the Master to his disciples, " The kingdom of God is in (among) you." Baptist polity is rapidly making way for this basic educational work as the churches clarify their vision in the presence of the Messiah whose Kingdom begins, progresses and ends in the world of spiritual values, heavenly qualities of life.

Clearer apprehension of the thought of the Master Teacher that the kingdom of God is here now, and in fact has always been here for those who would see and appropriate it, is giving a new potency to present-day evangelism. Men are appealed to by One who walks with both feet on the earth, who gives a spiritual interpretation of the universe and of the life within it, and who challenges them to enter here and now the Kingdom and fight to achieve its divine ends in their own souls and in the world. To sound this note of spiritual hopefulness, this message of good news, requires no change in the polity of the Baptist churches. The ways are already established, and hope of an enlarged service to the world of mankind lies with that increasing number of ministers whose passion, like that of their Lord, is for the prosperity of the Kingdom. The promise is of a new evangelism that calls for whole-hearted self-commitment to the life-changing and life-compelling dynamics of the Kingdom. Such is arising, and may be characterized as a vital rather than a mechanical evangelism.

Blessed indeed is that church that conceives its task to be the raising up of good citizens of the Kingdom; those in whose hearts the reign of God is operative; those, in other words, who have the Kingdom within them. The hope of the future lies with such. They are the salt of the earth and the light of the world. They are the city that cannot be hid, and whose glory, under Christ, shall fill the earth. Such men and women are tall and sun-crowned, good citizens of their respective communities, influential in every good cause, of whom all men boast because of the fairness of their minds, the purity of their motives and the generosity of their hearts. These are the colonists in that " colony of heaven " who are revealing that as the strength of the pack is in the wolf, so is the strength of the colony in the colonist. They give weight to the impact of the colony and carrying power to its influence. Let us repeat, happy is that church that concedes itself a failure except as it gives to Christ's Kingdom worthy citizens.

## The Kingdom and the Churches

By this test the Baptist churches have been fairly successful. They have given to the Christian world their share of princes of the Kingdom, and quite more than their share of those common men, the kingliness of whose lives are the heavenly leaven in any community. This is far from saying that their fruitage might not have been more excellent and more abundant; it is merely to make allowance for the inability of us ordinary human beings to attain those finer goals that rise before us. There are churches among us not unlike certain trees in an orchard, whose fruit is scrawny and sour, but those few do not condemn the whole orchard. There are ministers who are quarrelsome, ugly, petty, and obscurantist; and they produce fruit after their kind; fruit of no credit to the Kingdom; but these are exceptional and do not indict all who are honored to be preachers of Christ. Most of us have the genuine satisfaction of having helped to guide the growth of at least a few into a stature after the pattern of Jesus, and not unlike the "tree planted by the rivers of water" of the First Psalm.

Despite the splendor of its fruit, the Kingdom has its enemies; a fact so well known and so tragic as to need no reiteration. Would that it were unbelievable that those could be found who deliberately set themselves against the Father's reign in their hearts and their affairs. What shall the churches do concerning such men? Jesus' counsel in the parable of the Tares we have discussed. That counsel of moderation seems applicable to and wise for the local church. It is unthinkable that a church, bearing the name of Christ, should not oppose with vigor the forces of evil that aim to bring to naught the reign of God. On the other hand, it is undeniable folly for a church to be *consumed* in protest. The main task of a church is with a strong right arm to build the walls of the city of God, meanwhile keeping the enemies thereof at a safe distance. The pulpit must seek first to edify, to culture and enrich the people of the church, not neglecting to demand the rule of the righteousness of God in every social relationship. The polity of local independency and local self-government leaves each Baptist church free to choose its own manner of dealing with the enemies of the Kingdom. Some elect to ignore; others choose to be eternally in the fight, to make it their mission to raise the hue and cry, to sound the alarm. The people of the former group grow fat, soft and lazy, and become the dreamers of idle dreams; the latter grow thin and out of breath as they pant on the trail of wrong. The great majority of these independent churches avoid extremes, seek a wise and happy balance in their respective programs of service between the destructive and constructive tasks, and as a result they efficiently build their sector of the walls.

It is our conviction that our Baptist churches—among others—have not yet found an effective technique for proclaiming the social gospel. That the gospel which our Lord preached has all-inclusive social implications no one can deny; but how to get its salt at work is the problem. To herald it from the housetops, in season and out, is to alienate those whom one would win, namely, those men whose hands manipulate harmful social forces. Many preachers of the social gospel have erred by a technique of denunciation; a very poor technique at any time. Wiser men have become advocates before the jury, as it were, whose members they would win in behalf of the social righteousness of which the good Teacher spoke when he urged, " Seek ye first the kingdom of God and God's kind of righteousness, and other needful things will come along naturally." Perhaps the better way to get the social gospel over to where men live is by the narrowly educational method. Many classes in the church schools might give themselves, with great profit, to a discussion of vital social issues in the light of Kingdom ideals. Some classes are so engaged; and their number could readily be multiplied in most any church. Even from the younger ages the social demands of our Lord should confront both mind and heart. By every conceivable, legitimate means our churches must be instant in season and out of season to produce fruit for the kingdom of heaven, and its quality must reveal the flavor of both individual and social righteousness.

The foregoing pages in this chapter constitute a sort of harmony, written in two parallel columns. In the first we have set down the elemental and basic phases of the Kingdom; in the second we have indicated how a church, when it conceives its function with good understanding, relates itself to these primary demands. A study of the harmony thus written shows the right and proper relation of the Kingdom and the churches. In the first place, it is evident that the two are not identical, as is sometimes assumed. The former is an ideal, spiritual in content, and found in the process of realization, while the churches are very practical, work-a-day institutions, creations of this present material world. Far from identical, indeed, yet vitally related, are the two; related as creator and created, cause and effect. The Kingdom ideal, when passed through the personality of Jesus Christ, became a social dynamic, and this in turn gave birth to the church. But to what end, one may ask? This, that the churches might harness the power of the ideal and direct its creativity so as to actualize in the world the reign of the divine, to establish the kingdom of God. Hence *the churches are a means to an end,* the instrument by operation of which the Kingdom that our Lord dreamed about is to be made real. They are his to employ in making his dream come true, the dream of a world order wherein all men and institutions should be under the sway of God the Father. Happily, the fluid polity of the Baptist churches makes it possible for them to remain supple in his hand and ready thereby to help forward the changing phases of that kingdom of God which at once is coming down from heaven and growing up from among the people. Blessed are those churches that are found helping him bring to consummation in human hearts and in the social order the things which, as Saint Luke says, " he began both to do and teach."

### TOPICS FOR GROUP DISCUSSION

1. After making a careful study of the life and work of John the Baptist, by free group discussion determine the rôle he played in the unfolding drama of the kingdom of God.

2. As the ideal for his own life and ministry as well as for that of his disciples, what content did Jesus put into the kingdom of God idea?

3. Resolved, that the Kingdom, as our Lord conceived it, primarily looks toward a righteous social order on the earth.

4. Assuming that Jesus Christ dreamed of an *ecclesia,* or church, what, in view of the kingdom of God ideal, must he have conceived the main function of that church to be?

5. By discussion create a composite picture of a good and true citizen of the kingdom of God; the outline of his character; his major interests; his manner of living, and his contribution toward the coming of the Kingdom in his own community.

6. Are the churches the divinely ordained means toward an end, namely the establishment of the kingdom of God among men? Or are they the end itself?

## Books Worth Consulting

Beers, G. Pitt, *Ministry to Turbulent America.* The Judson Press, Philadelphia, 1957.

Harnack, Adolph. *What Is Christianity?* Harper and Brothers, New York, 1957.

Klemms, Huber F., *Your Church and Your Community.* Christian Education Press, Philadelphia, 1957.

Landis, Benson Y., compiler, *A Rauschenbusch Reader: The Kingdom of God and the Social Gospel.* Harper and Brothers, New York, 1957.

Payne, Ernest A., *The Fellowship of Believers: Baptist Thought and Practice Yesterday and Today.* The Kingsgate Press, London, 1945.

Rasmussen, Albert Terrill, *Christian Social Ethics Exerting Christian Influence.* Prentice-Hall, Inc., Englewood Cliffs, N. J., 1956.

Younger, George D., *The Bible Calls for Action.* The Judson Press, Philadelphia, 1959.

## Practical Suggestions

1. Make a study of ten churches known to your group, ascertaining whether or not the type of preaching and

teaching in each fosters and furthers the kingdom of God as Christ proclaimed it. Is the aim of these churches to secure for men a safe entrance into heaven? Or rather to grow men who are worthy citizens of the Kingdom? Do they aim to get men into heaven " by and by," or to get heaven into men now so that they will do something about Kingdom expansion among the peoples?

2. Make a comparative study of the Year-Books of the various denominations, with a view to discovering expressed denominational aims, and whether or not these obey our Lord Jesus Christ when he urges, " Seek ye first the kingdom of God and God's kind of righteousness."

# APPENDIX

## SUGGESTED CONSTITUTION for BAPTIST CHURCHES[1]

### ARTICLE I.—NAME

The name of this church shall be the _____
Baptist Church of _____

### ARTICLE II.—PURPOSE

The purpose of this church shall be the advancement of the Kingdom of Jesus Christ. It shall seek to attain this end through the public worship of God, the preaching of the Gospel, consistent Christian living by its members, personal evangelism, missionary endeavor and Christian education.

### ARTICLE III.—POLITY

Its government shall be vested in the body which composes its membership. It shall, however, maintain affiliation and cooperation with the _____ Association, the
_____ State Convention and the American Baptist Convention.

### ARTICLE IV.—DOCTRINE

This church receives the New Testament as an all sufficient basis of doctrine and practice. As a summary of principles for Christian conduct among its members it adopts the following church covenant commonly accepted by Baptist churches.

### CHURCH COVENANT

Having been led, as we believe, by the Spirit of God, to receive the Lord Jesus Christ as our Saviour, and on the profession of our faith, having been baptized in the name of the Father, and of the Son, and of the Holy Spirit, we do now in the presence of God and this assembly, most solemnly and joyfully enter into covenant with one another, as one body in Christ.

---

[1] Johnson, Ralph M. and Goodwin, R. Dean, *Faith and Fellowship of American Baptists.* Council on Missionary Cooperation of the American Baptist Convention, New York, 1957.

# *Appendix*

We engage, therefore, by the aid of the Holy Spirit, to walk together in Christian love; to strive for the advancement of this church in knowledge, holiness and comfort; to promote its prosperity and spirituality; to sustain its worship, ordinances, discipline and doctrines, to contribute cheerfully and regularly to the support of the ministry, the expenses of the church, the relief of the poor and the spread of the Gospel through all nations.

We also engage to maintain family and secret devotions; to teach our children the Christian truths; to seek the salvation of our kindred and acquaintances; to walk circumspectly in the world; to be just in our dealings, faithful in our engagements, exemplary in our deportment; to avoid all tattling, backbiting and excessive anger; to abstain from the sale and use of intoxicating drink as beverage; and to be zealous in our efforts to advance the Kingdom of our Saviour.

We further engage to watch over one another in brotherly love; to remember each other in prayer; to aid each other in sickness and distress; to cultivate Christian sympathy in feeling and courtesy in speech; to be slow to take offense but always ready for reconciliation, and mindful of the rules of our Saviour to secure it without delay.

We moreover engage that when we remove from this place, we will as soon as possible unite with some other church where we can carry out the spirit of the covenant and principles of God's Word.

## ARTICLE V.—MEMBERSHIP

SECTION 1. *Admission of Members.* The members of this church shall consist of persons professing faith in the Lord Jesus Christ, giving evidence of a changed heart followed by immersion and accepting the faith and practice held by the church.*

*By Baptism.* A person who confesses Jesus Christ as Lord and Saviour and adopts substantially the views of faith and principles of this church and is baptized by immersion may be received into the fellowship of the church.

*By Letter.* A person who is in substantial accord with the views of faith and the principles of this church may be received by letter from any other Baptist Church.*

*By Experience.* A believer of worthy character who has formerly been a member of a Baptist church but who, for a sufficient rea-

# *Appendix*

son, cannot present a letter from that church but who is in substantial accord with the views of faith and principles of this church may be received upon statement of experience.*

*By Restoration.* A person who has lost his membership may be restored to membership upon recommendation of the board of deacons and vote of the church.

Sec. 2. *Dismissal of Members.*

*By Letter.* Any member in good standing who desires a letter of dismission and recommendation to any other Baptist church may receive it upon his request and upon the recommendation of the board of deacons and vote of the church. The name of the church to which membership is requested shall be named in the request and the letter shall be sent to the pastor or clerk of that church. Such letter shall be valid only for six months after its date, unless renewed, and this restriction shall be stated in the letter.

*By Statement.* Any member in good standing may be granted a certificate of standing for the purpose of associating himself with any evangelical church other than a Baptist church.

*By Exclusion.* Should any member become an offense to the church and to its good name by reason of immoral or unchristian conduct, or by consistent breach of his covenant vows, the church may terminate his membership, but only after due notice and a hearing before the board of deacons, and after faithful efforts have been made to bring such member to repentance and amendment.

*By Suspension.* The board of deacons should prepare, from year to year, a list of those members who have for a period of two or more years failed to participate in the service of worship or financial support of the church without valid excuse. If they are satisfied that the persons so described cannot be reclaimed, they shall present to the church a recommendation that these delinquent members be erased from the membership roll. Upon such action being taken by the church, said members shall thereafter cease to be members of this church.

* (Note: Some churches provide for associate membership. In such cases the person may be received by letter or experience from some other evangelical church. Associate members shall be entitled to all the rights and privileges of the church except that they shall not be allowed to vote on matters that determine the church's relationship to the American Baptist Convention. The church administers baptism by immersion only.)

# *Appendix*

## ARTICLE VI.—THE PASTOR AND OFFICERS

Section 1. *Pastor.* The pastor shall preach the Gospel, administer the ordinances, watch over the membership, have in his charge the spiritual welfare of the congregation and the stated services of public worship. He shall be an ex-officio member of all boards and committees of the church and its auxiliary organizations.

Sec. 2. *Moderator.* The moderator shall preside at all business meetings of the church and at all meetings of the advisory council when the pastor is absent. He shall be elected at each annual meeting to serve for one year.

Sec. 3. *Clerk.* A clerk shall be elected at each annual meeting to serve for one year. He shall keep a complete record of the transaction of all business at the meetings of the church. This shall be read for approval at the next following business meeting. He shall keep a record of the names and addresses of members, with dates and manner of admission and dismission; also a record of baptisms and a list of those suspended. He shall notify all officers, committee members and delegates of their election and appointment. He shall issue letters of dismission and recommendation voted by the church, preserve on file all communications and written reports, and give legal notice of all meetings where such is required by this constitution. He shall assist in preparing denominational reports. He shall deliver immediately to his successor all books and records for which he has been responsible as clerk.

Sec. 4. *Local Expense Treasurer.* A local expense treasurer shall be elected at each annual meeting to serve for one year. He shall have custody of the funds of the church and all deposits made in the name of the church, and all checks drawn by him shall be in the name of the church. He shall keep separate accounts of all funds raised or contributed for particular purposes, and no funds shall be disbursed by him except for the purposes for which they were raised or contributed. He shall have custody of the securities, investments, title papers and other valuable documents of the church.

Funds received for the support of the church, and for the reduction of the church indebtedness, shall be disbursed by him only on the order of the board of trustees.

# *Appendix*

He shall present to the church an itemized report of receipts and disbursements, showing the actual financial condition of the church at each annual meeting, this report to have been audited previously by the auditors elected by the church. He shall make such other financial reports as may be desired by the church.

He shall deliver immediately to his successor all books and records pertaining to his office.

SEC. 5. *Benevolence Treasurer.* A benevolence treasurer shall be elected at each annual meeting to serve for one year. He shall pay over, monthly, all funds received on account of the church's contribution to the benevolent purposes of the American Baptist Convention and its affiliates. Other benevolence funds shall be applied by him in accordance with the church budget and the special purposes for which the same were contributed.

He shall present to the church an itemized report of receipts and disbursements, showing the actual financial condition of the church at each annual meeting, this report to have been audited previously by the auditors elected by the church. He shall make such other financial reports as may be desired by the church.

He shall deliver immediately to his successor all books and records pertaining to his office.

SEC. 6. *Financial Secretary.* A financial secretary shall be elected at each annual meeting to serve for one year. It shall be his duty to furnish each member of the church envelopes for contribution to church expense and benevolence; to keep a record of all pledges made; to collect all moneys contributed and to keep a correct account thereof between the church and its members. He shall deposit such collections weekly, in the bank selected by the board of trustees, and render a statement thereof to the treasurer. He shall, at the end of each fiscal year, report to the board of trustees an account of the matters pertaining to his office and report to the board of deacons the names of those members who have failed to make any contributions of record toward church expense or benevolence. This officer acts as a receiving agent for funds contributed for causes within the American Baptist Convention. Individual members contributing to outside agencies should do so directly.

SEC. 7. *The Superintendent of the Church School.* At each annual meeting of the church a superintendent of the church school shall be elected for a term of one year. He shall be the executive head of the church school, exercising the authority and performing the duties usually pertaining to that office, following the general directives and policies of the board of Christian education.

## ARTICLE VII.—ADVISORY COUNCIL

There shall be an advisory council consisting of the elected officers of the church, members of boards* and chairmen of all standing committees, and presidents of all auxiliary organizations. All matters of importance should be considered by it before being presented to the church. It shall appoint, subject to ratification by the church, all standing committees. It shall seek to coordinate the activities of the church. It shall be instrumental in developing a program for the church, including long-range planning. The council shall undertake to strengthen the total work of the church, its boards, committees and auxiliary organizations. As a representative group it should serve as the program and proposal committee during the period prior to the financial enlistment. It should appoint the Every Member Canvass Committee, the auditing committee and other standing and special committees.

The advisory council shall arrange for an annual every member canvass for the current expenses and benevolences of the church which shall be held in March or November. A representative committee shall be appointed to prepare a proposed goal for the every member canvass. This proposal committee shall have representatives from the various boards and auxiliary organizations of the church. This proposed goal shall be presented to the church for adoption as a goal before the canvass.

## ARTICLE VIII.—BOARDS

Section 1. *The Board of Deacons.* There shall be a board of (3, 6, 9, or 12) deacons, one-third of whom shall be elected from the membership of the church at each annual meeting for a term of three years. Consecutive terms shall be limited to two.

The board shall choose annually a chairman, a secretary and

---

* Larger churches may find it preferable to include only the chairman and a few elected members of the boards.

# *Appendix*

a treasurer and shall meet regularly each month. Special meetings my be called by the chairman or the secretary, who shall notify the other members. A majority of the members shall constitute a quorum.

The board shall in every way assist the pastor in his work; with him consider all applicants for church membership and all requests for letters of dismission; cooperate with him in providing the pulpit supply and the leaders of the prayer meeting in his absence; visit the members; care for the sick, needy and distressed members of the church, using such fellowship funds as may be needed.

The board shall promote Christian instruction and ministry to the church membership, provide for the Lord's Supper and aid in its administration; deliver to the treasurer the fellowship offering received at each communion service; and make a written report at each annual meeting of the church on the matters in its charge.

Sec. 2. *Deaconesses.* (See Deacons.)

Sec. 3. *The Board of Trustees.* There shall be a board of (3, 6, 9, or 12) trustees, one-third of whom shall be elected at each annual meeting for a term of three years. Consecutive terms shall be limited to two. The clerk, treasurer and financial secretary shall have the privilege of attending its meetings and shall be present when so requested by the board.

The board shall choose annually a chairman and a secretary and shall meet regularly each month. Special meetings may be called by the chairman or by the secretary, who shall notify the other members. A majority of the members shall constitute a quorum.

The board shall hold in trust all property belonging to the church and shall take all necessary measures for its protection, management and upkeep. It shall determine the use of the church building for all extra or secular purposes, but it shall have no power to buy, mortgage, lease or transfer any property without specific vote of the church authorizing such action. It shall designate the bank where the funds of the church shall be deposited. All bills authorized by the church shall be approved by the board before payment is made. It shall, when so instructed by the church, secure the services of a caretaker at such salary as is authorized by the church and secure from him acceptable service. It shall perform such other duties as are imposed upon it by the church and the state.

The board shall supervise ways and means of raising the necessary funds for the support of the church and for benevolences, either itself or through a representative every member enlistment committee. It shall supervise the disbursement of these funds as appropriated. It shall make written reports to the church at the annual meeting and at such other times as may be desired. Following the canvass a budget of current expenses shall be set up.

SEC. 4. *The Board of Christian Education.* There shall be a board of Christian education composed of (3, 6, or 9) members, one-third of whom shall be elected at each annual meeting for a term of three years.

The board shall be organized promptly following the annual election. It shall select from its own membership a chairman, vice-chairman, and secretary. It shall meet monthly at a stated time. Special meetings may be called by the chairman at any time and shall be called upon the request of the pastor. A quorum shall consist of ——— elected members (usually a majority of the board). The secretary of the board shall notify the members of all meetings, enter accurate minutes of the meetings in a book to be kept for that purpose, have custody of and be responsible for all books, papers and documents pertaining to the affairs of the board, and surrender all records to the board when a new secretary is elected. The board shall prepare a report of the year's Christian education program, budget and activities for presentation at the annual meeting of the church.

The board shall be responsible for the organization and administration of the entire educational program of the church. It shall be responsible for developing and interpreting to the constituency of the church the educational objectives or goals. It shall be responsible for studying the educational needs of the church and for making decisions concerning (1) time schedule, (2) educational use of housing and equipment, and (3) the elimination or addition of classes or organizations. It shall be responsible for discovering, enlisting, training and appointing all church educational workers. It shall be responsible for evaluating and supervising the curriculum of the educational program. It shall be responsible for coordinating and approving the out-reach programs of the groups and organizations under its jurisdiction, such as home-church, community relationship, and educational programs in cooperation with other churches are included in this responsibility. It shall be responsible for preparing and administering the education budget of the church.

SEC. 5. *The Board of Missionary Promotion.* There shall be a Board of Missionary Promotion of (3, 5, 7, or 9) members one-third of whom shall be elected at each annual meeting for a term of three years. Following the church financial canvass a missionary budget shall be set up by the Board of Missionary Promotion after consultation with the Advisory Council for adoption as a working budget and presented for adoption by the church at the annual meeting.

The board shall seek to increase missionary interest and giving to the total work of the American Baptist Convention by general promotion and special events, missionary speakers, missionary films, and projects to personalize missions. The board shall promote cooperation with other churches in the association and convention, in the furthering of missionary enterprises.

In the field of home missions, the board shall have the responsibility of starting and administering mission projects that may develop into self-supporting churches.

The board shall seek to correlate and encourage the missionary activity of the woman's society, the men's fellowship, the B.Y.F. and other organized groups in the church. An ex-officio member of this board shall be a member of the missionary and stewardship education committee of the board of education.

SEC. 6. *Office Tenure.* After a church member has held office for two consecutive terms (or one term) in any one of the above boards he shall not be eligible for re-election to the same office for a period of one year after the expiration of the second term (or that term).

No person shall hold more than one of the above offices at the same time except the Moderator.

# *Appendix*

## ARTICLE IX.—COMMITTEES

SECTION 1. *Evangelism Committee.* The evangelism committee shall be a committee of representative membership, appointed by the advisory council. It shall cooperate with the pastor in arranging for special evangelistic meetings, visitation evangelism and printed page evangelism.

SEC. 2. *Committee on Missionary Promotion.* (When there is no board of missionary promotion.) The committee on missionary promotion shall help the church accept and reach a high goal of missionary giving. It shall cooperate with state and national groups on missionary cooperation to promote giving and in general seek to do the work of a board of missionary promotion.

SEC. 3. *Communications.* The communications committee, appointed by the advisory council, shall make known the church, what it stands for and what it has to offer, by the use of newspapers, radio, television and other available media.

SEC. 4. *Christian Social Education and Action Committee.* Christian social education and action committee, appointed by the advisory council and representative of the total church body, shall give leadership in programs to alert the congregation to their wider responsibilities as Christian citizens.

SEC. 5. *Social Committee.* The social committee, appointed by the advisory council, shall promote fellowship within the church. It shall help members become better acquainted.

SEC. 6. *Music Committee.* The music committee, appointed by the advisory council, shall cooperate with the pastor in the selection of an organist and choir director and in the arrangement of the music of the church services. It shall incur expense only as authorized by the church.

SEC. 7. *Ushering Committee.* The ushering committee, appointed by the advisory council, shall attend to the seating of the congregation and to the receiving of the offering, except as otherwise provided.

SEC. 8. *Nominating Committee.* The nominating committee shall be appointed by the Advisory Council following the annual meeting of the church. It shall serve through the next annual meeting. It shall prepare a list of those qualified to fill the various offices. It shall interview each nominee proposed and ascertain his or her willingness to serve if elected. The committee shall nominate one or more persons for each office to be filled and report the names to the church at least one week before the election is to be held.

SEC. 9. *Every Member Canvass Committee.* The every member canvass committee shall have the responsibility of conducting the every member canvass. It shall be appointed by and report to the advisory council.

SEC. 10. *Auditing Committee.* The auditing committee, appointed by the advisory council, shall audit the financial records of the church at least once each year and shall make a report in writing to the church at the time of the annual meeting.

SEC. 11. *Pulpit Committee.* When the pastorate is vacant, a pulpit committee composed of five (or more) members of the church, representing all groups, shall be nominated to the church by the advisory council. This committee shall take the necessary steps to secure a pastor in full consultation with a state or city secretary of the American Baptist Convention. It shall investigate the merits of each candidate under consideration in regard to his personal character, education, ministerial record, and preaching ability in determining his fitness for this pastorate. When a suitable person is found the committee shall recommend him to the church for consideration.

SEC. 12. *Special and General Committees.* Special committees shall be appointed by the advisory council as need shall arise. The principle of rotation in effect for boards shall apply to committees and committee chairmen.

### ARTICLE X.—THE PASTORATE

SECTION 1. *Calling a pastor.* The call of a pastor shall come before the church at a regularly called business meeting, notice of such meeting and its purpose having been read from the pulpit on two successive Sundays. Only a man who is sympathetically cooperative with the purposes and program of the American Baptist Convention shall be considered. A vote of three-fourths of the members present and qualified to vote, provided there be

# Appendix

present and voting _____ members, shall be necessary to extend a call.

Only one candidate shall be presented to the church at one time. The vote shall be by written ballot.

SEC. 2. *Termination of Pastorate.* The term of office may be ended upon at least thirty days' notice on the part of the pastor or of the church or by mutual consent.

Termination of the office shall be voted at a regularly called business meeting, notice of such meeting and its purpose having been read from the pulpit on two successive Sundays. A vote of a majority of the members present and qualified to vote, provided there be present and voting _____ members, shall make valid termination of said office.

## ARTICLE XI.—ELECTIONS

SECTION 1. *Time.* The annual election of officers shall be held during the annual meeting of the church which shall be on the second _____ evening in December (or January).

SEC. 2. *Qualifications of Voters.* All matters pertaining to the purchase, sale or mortgaging of property shall be voted on only by members in good standing and who are of legal age. On all other matters members in good standing who are fifteen years of age or older are entitled to vote.

SEC. 3. *Procedure.* At least one week before the election the nominating committee shall present to the church the names of one or more persons for each office to be filled. At the time of the annual meeting it shall be the privilege of any member present and qualified to vote to place in nomination the name of any eligible person for any office not so nominated. A majority of the ballots cast are necessary for the election of any officer.

SEC. 4. *Vacancies.* Vacancies occurring during the year may be filled for the unexpired term at any business meeting. The nominating committee shall present to the church nominees for the vacancy to be filled.

## ARTICLE XII.—MEETINGS

SECTION 1. *Worship Service.* Public services shall be on each

[ 256 ]

# Appendix

Lord's Day and the youth fellowships and the church school shall hold weekly meetings at times fixed by the Board of Education and approved by the Advisory Council and the church.

The Lord's Supper shall be celebrated on the first Sunday morning of each month, and at such other times as the church may determine.

Occasional religious meetings may be appointed by the pastor at his discretion, by the advisory council, or by vote of the church.

SEC. 2. *Business Meetings.* The annual business meeting shall be on the second _____ evening in December (or January) for the purpose of receiving the annual reports of individual officers, boards and committees of the church and its auxiliary organizations; the election of officers; and the transaction of such other business as is proper to come before this meeting. Quarterly business meetings shall be held in (January), April, July and October.

A quorum for the transaction of business shall be _____.

Special business meetings may be called at any time by the pastor or by the clerk or by five members in good standing who are qualified voters. Notice of such meeting and the object for which it is called shall be given from the pulpit on the Sunday preceding the date of the meeting. At any of the regular meetings of worship, however, the church may, without notice, act upon the reception of members, upon the dismission of members to other churches, and upon the appointment of delegates to councils, associations and conventions, but not upon extraordinary business.

## ARTICLE XIII.—CHURCH YEAR

The fiscal year of the church shall be the calendar year.

## ARTICLE XIV.—AMENDMENTS

This constitution may be amended at any regular or called business meeting of the church by a two-thirds vote of those present and voting, provided a quorum is present and voting, and that notice of such amendment, stating the proposed change, shall have been given from the pulpit on two successive Sundays.

# BIBLIOGRAPHY

Agar, Frederick A., *The Deacon at Work*. The Judson Press, Philadelphia, 1923.

Asquith, Glenn, *Church Officers at Work*. The Judson Press, Philadelphia, 1951; revised 1952.

Baillie, Donald M. and Marsh, John, eds., *Intercommunion*. Harper and Brothers, New York, 1952.

Baptist, The, vol. 7, pp. 649, 650; 1926, *Where, Then, Does Authority Lie?*

Beers, G. Pitt, *Ministry to Turbulent America*. The Judson Press, Philadelphia, 1957.

Berkeley, James P., *You Can Teach*. The Judson Press, Philadelphia, 1941.

Bilheimer, Robert S., *The Quest for Christian Unity*. The Association Press, New York, 1952.

Blankenship, Lois, *Our Church Plans for Children*. The Judson Press, Philadelphia, 1952; revised 1958.

Bowman, Clarice, *Ways Youth Learn*. Harper and Brothers, New York, 1952.

Bromiley, G. W., *Baptism and the Anglican Reformers*. The Lutterworth Press, London, 1953.

Brown, Jeannette Perkins, *The Storyteller in Religious Education*. The Pilgrim Press, Boston, 1951.

Brown, Kenneth I., ". . . *And Be Baptized*." The Judson Press, Philadelphia, 1952.

Butt, Elsie Miller, *The Vacation School in Religious Education*. The Abingdon Press, Nashville, 1957.

Caldwell, Irene S., *Adults Learn and Like It*. Warner Press, Anderson, Indiana, 1956.

Champion, L. G., *The Church of the New Testament*. The Kingsgate Press, London, 1951.

Clark, Wayne C., *The Meaning of Church Membership*. The Judson Press, Philadelphia, 1950.

Cober, Kenneth L., *Evangelism in the Sunday Church School*. The Judson Press, Philadelphia, 1955.

# Bibliography

Coffin, Henry Sloane, *Communion Through Preaching.* Charles Scribner's Sons, New York, 1952.

Cook, Henry, *What Baptists Stand For.* The Kingsgate Press, London, 1947.

Crossland, Weldon, *Better Leaders for Your Church.* The Abingdon Press, Nashville, 1955.

Cummings, Oliver deWolf, *The Youth Fellowship.* The Judson Press, Philadelphia, 1956.

Davies, Horton, *Christian Worship—Its History and Meaning.* The Abingdon Press, Nashville, 1957.

Dolloff, Eugene Dinsmore, *The Efficient Church Officer: His Responsibilities and Problems.* Fleming H. Revell Co., New York, 1949.

Eakin, Mildred Moody and Eakin, Frank, *The Church-School Teacher's Job.* The Macmillan Co., New York, 1949.

Encyclopedia Britannica

Fahs, Sophia L. and Manwell, Elizabeth, *Consider the Children.* The Beacon Press, Inc., Boston, 1951.

Ferré, Nels F. S., *Christian Fellowship.* Harper and Brothers, New York, 1940.

Fordham, Forrest B., *Our Church Plans for Youth.* The Judson Press, Philadelphia, 1953.

Fosdick, Harry Emerson, *The Modern Use of the Bible.* The Macmillan Co., New York, 1941.

Garrison, Winfred E., *The Quest and Character of a United Church.* The Abingdon Press, Nashville, 1957.

Goodspeed, Edgar J., *The Story of the New Testament.* The University of Chicago Press, Chicago, 1931.

Goodwin, R. Dean, *Man: Living Soul.* The Judson Press, Philadelphia, 1952.

Handy, Robert T., *We Witness Together.* The Friendship Press, New York, 1956.

Harnack, Adolph, *What Is Christianity?* Harper and Brothers, New York, 1957.

Hastings, James, *Encyclopedia of Religion and Ethics,* 13 vols. Charles Scribner's Sons, New York, 1951.

# Bibliography

Hill, Frances and Stansbury, Florence, *The Missionary Education of Children.* The Judson Press, Philadelphia, 1954.

Hiscox, Edward T., *The Standard Manual for Baptist Churches.* The Judson Press, Philadelphia, 1890.

——————, *The New Directory for Baptist Churches.* The Judson Press, Philadelphia, 1894.

——————, *The Star Book for Ministers.* The Judson Press, Philadelphia, 1878.

Hoiland, Richard, *Planning Christian Education in the Local Church.* The Judson Press, Philadelphia; revised 1952.

Hovey, Alvah, *The Seat of Authority.* The *Watchman,* Sept. 18, 1902.

Ivison, Stuart and Rosser, Fred, *Baptists in Upper and Lower Canada Before 1820.* University of Toronto Press, Toronto, 1956.

Jenkins, Daniel T., *Congregationalism: A Restatement.* Harper and Brothers, New York, 1954.

——————, *The Strangeness of the Church.* Doubleday and Co., Inc., Garden City, 1955.

Johnson, Ralph M. and Goodwin, R. Dean, *Faith and Fellowship of American Baptists.* Council on Missionary Cooperation of the American Baptist Convention, New York, 1957.

Jones, Idris, *Our Church Plans for Adult Education.* The Judson Press, Philadelphia, 1953.

——————, *The Superintendent Plans His Work.* The Judson Press, Philadelphia, 1956.

Kautsky, Karl, *The Foundations of Christianity.* S. A. Russell, New York, 1953.

Keighton, Robert E., *The Minister's Communion Service Book.* The Judson Press, Philadelphia, 1947.

Kirk, Kenneth E., *The Apostolic Ministry.* Morehouse-Gorham Co., New York, 1946.

Klemms, Huber F., *Your Church and Your Community.* Christian Education Press, Philadelphia, 1957.

Knudsen, Ralph E., *Christian Beliefs.* The Judson Press, Philadelphia, 1947.

# Bibliography

Lamott, Willis C., *Revolutions in Missions*. The Macmillan Co., New York, 1954.

Landis, Benson Y., compiler, *A Rauschenbusch Reader: The Kingdom of God and the Social Gospel*. Harper and Brothers, New York, 1957.

Latourette, Kenneth Scott, *Toward a World Christian Fellowship*. The Association Press, New York, 1938.

——————, *The Emergence of a World Christian Community*. Yale University Press, New Haven, 1949.

——————, *A History of Christianity*. Harper and Brothers, New York, 1953.

——————, *The Christian World Mission in Our Day*. Harper and Brothers, New York, 1954.

Leavenworth, Lynn, ed., *Great Themes in Theology*. The Judson Press, Philadelphia, 1958.

Levy, George Edward, *The Baptists of the Maritime Provinces, 1753-1946*. Barnes-Hopkins, Ltd., St. John, N.B., 1946.

Little, Sarah, *Learning Together in the Christian Fellowship*. John Knox Press, Richmond, 1956.

Lobinger, John Leslie, *If Teaching Is Your Job*. The Pilgrim Press, Boston, 1956.

Lotz, Philip Henry, ed., *Orientation in Religious Education*. The Abingdon Press, Nashville, 1950.

Lumpkin, William L., *Baptist Confessions of Faith*. The Judson Press, Philadelphia, 1959.

Maves, Paul B. and Cedarleaf, J. Lennart, *Older People and the Church*. The Abingdon Press, Nashville, 1949.

Maxwell, W. D., *Outline of Christian Worship; Its Development and Forms*. Oxford University Press, New York, 1940.

Maynard, Donald M., *Your Home Can Be Christian*. The Abingdon Press, Nashville, 1952.

McCall, Duke K., ed., *What Is the Church? A Symposium of Baptist Thought*. The Broadman Press, Nashville, 1958.

McConnell, F. M., *McConnell's Manual for Baptist Churches*. The Judson Press, Philadelphia, 1926.

# Bibliography

Miller, Randolph Crump, *Biblical Theology and Christian Education.* Charles Scribner's Sons, New York, 1956.

————, *Education for Christian Living.* Prentice-Hall, Inc., New York, 1956.

Morsch, Vivian Sharp, *The Use of Music in Religious Education.* The Westminster Press, Philadelphia, 1956.

Mullins, Edgar Y., *Baptist Beliefs.* The Judson Press, Philadelphia, 1925.

————, *The Axioms of Religion.* The American Baptist Publication Society, Philadelphia, 1908.

Nelson, John Oliver, *Young Laymen—Young Church.* Association Press, New York, 1948.

Newbigin, Leslie, *The Household of God: Lectures on the Nature of the Church.* The Friendship Press, New York, 1954.

Newman, Albert H., *A History of the Baptist Churches in the United States.* The American Baptist Publication Society, Philadelphia, 1898.

————, *A Manual of Church History.* The Judson Press, Philadelphia, 1903.

Otto, Rudolf (translated by J. W. Harvey), *The Idea of the Holy.* Oxford University Press, New York, 2nd edition, 1950.

Payne, Ernest A., *The Fellowship of Believers: Baptist Thought and Practice Yesterday and Today.* The Kingsgate Press, London, 1945.

Peck, A. L., *This Church of Christ.* Morehouse-Gorham Co., New York, 1955.

Phillips, J. B., *Appointment with God.* The Macmillan Co., New York, 1954.

Pittenger, W. Norman, *The Church, The Ministry, and Reunion.* The Seabury Press, Inc., Greenwich, Conn., 1957.

Rasmussen, Albert Terrill, *Christian Social Ethics Exerting Christian Influence.* Prentice-Hall, Inc., Englewood Cliffs, N. J., 1956.

Robinson, William, *The Biblical Doctrine of the Church.* The Bethany Press, St. Louis, 1955.

# Bibliography

Schaff, Philip, *History of the Christian Church,* 8 vols. The William B. Eerdmans Co., Grand Rapids, 1950.

Schaff, Philip and Herzog, Johann, *The Schaff-Herzog Encyclopedia of Religious Knowledge,* 15 vols. Baker Book House, Grand Rapids, 1955.

Shaver, Erwin L., *The Weekday Church School.* The Pilgrim Press, Boston, 1956.

Smart, James D., *The Teaching Ministry of the Church.* The Westminster Press, Philadelphia, 1954.

Smith, Gerald B., *The Principles of Christian Living,* 2nd edition revised by Leland Foster Wood. The University of Chicago Press, Chicago, 1942.

Smith, Miles W., *On Whom the Spirit Came.* The Judson Press, Philadelphia, 1948.

Stevens, Dorothy, *Missionary Education in a Baptist Church.* The Judson Press, Philadelphia, 1953.

Straton, Hillyer H., *Baptists: Their Messsage and Mission.* The Judson Press, Philadelphia, 1941.

Strong, Augustus Hopkins, *Systematic Theology.* The Judson Press, Philadelphia, 1907.

Stuber, Stanley I., *How We Got Our Denominations.* Association Press, New York, 1948.

Sweet, William Warren, ed., *Religion on the American Frontier,* 4 vols., Vol. I, *The Baptists, 1783-1830.* Henry Holt and Co., New York, 1931.

——————, *The Story of Religion in America.* Harper and Brothers, New York; revised, 1939.

——————, *Religion in Colonial America.* Charles Scribner's Sons, New York, 1942.

——————, *Revivalism in America: Its Origin, Growth, and Decline.* Charles Scribner's Sons, New York, 1944.

Torbet, Robert G., *A History of the Baptists.* The Judson Press, Philadelphia, 1950; revised 1955.

——————, *The Baptist Ministry: Then and Now.* The Judson Press, Philadelphia, 1953.

# Bibliography

Torbet, Robert G., *The Baptist Story*. The Judson Press, Philadelphia, 1957.

Tower, Howard E., *The Church Use of Audio-Visuals*. The Abingdon Press, Nashville, 1951.

Trueblood, Elton, *The Common Ventures of Life*. Harper and Brothers, New York, 1949.

Underwood, A. C., *A History of the English Baptists*. The Kingsgate Press, London, 1947.

Vedder, Henry C., *A Short History of the Baptists*. The American Baptist Publication Society, Philadelphia, 1907.

Walton, Robert C., *The Gathered Community*. The Carey Press, London, 1946.

Whitehouse, Elizabeth, *The Children We Teach*. The Judson Press, Philadelphia, 1950.

—————, *Opening the Bible to Children*. The Bethany Press, St. Louis; revised 1955.

Wise, B. Fred, ed., *Christian Worship, A Hymnal*. The Judson Press, Philadelphia, 1955.

Wygal, Winnifred, *How to Plan Informal Worship*. The Association Press, New York, 1955.

Yeaxlee, Basil A., *Religion and the Growing Mind*. The Seabury Press, Inc.; revised 1952.

# INDEX

# Index